T0244675

YOU CAN'T TEACH AN OLD DOG NEW TRICKS

YOU CAN'T TEACH AN OLD DOG NEW TRICKS

Harry Dixon

Michael O'Mara Books Limited

First published in Great Britain in 2024 by
Michael O'Mara Books Limited
9 Lion Yard
Tremadoc Road
London SW4 7NQ

A CIP catalogue record for this book is available from the British
Library.

This product is made of material from well-managed, FSC®-certified
forests and other controlled sources. The manufacturing processes
conform to the environmental regulations of the country of origin.

ISBN: 978-1-78929-631-0 in hardback print format
ISBN: 978-1-78929-691-4 in ebook format

1 2 3 4 5 6 7 8 9 10

Designed and typeset by D23
Illustrations by Andrew Pinder
Jacket photograph from Shutterstock
Printed and bound by CPI Group (UK) Ltd, Croydon, CR0 4YY
www.mombooks.com

Contents

Introduction

They say that you can't teach an old dog new tricks. But is that really true? If you are over the age of forty, have a think about all the new tricks you have had to learn in your lifetime. Depending how long ago your fortieth birthday was, you have had to get accustomed to a huge number of discombobulating new phenomena, including, but not limited to:

- The reality of humans travelling in space
- The 'sexual revolution'
- The switch to decimal currency
- Britain joining the European Economic Community
- The rise of cheap air travel and package holidays
- The decline of industrial Britain and rise of the 'service economy'
- Disco music, punk music, electronic music ...
- Home computers
- The fax machine
- Mobile phones

YOU CAN'T TEACH AN OLD DOG NEW TRICKS

- The Internet
- Email communication
- Throwing out the fax machine
- No smoking in pubs
- The Big Bang in financial services
- A string of financial bubbles, crashes and booms
- Tourists flying to space
- Online banking
- Social media
- Britain leaving the European Union
- Pandemics, face masks and vaccines
- Working from home
- Zoom meetings
- The cost of living crisis
- The rise of Artificial Intelligence (AI)

This list could continue for pages. We have lived through a period of constant upheaval, ongoing invention, creative destruction and obsolescence, and relentless technological progress, which has made life easier in some ways, and infinitely more infuriating in others. So these old dogs have already learned plenty of new tricks, thank you very much.

But it keeps on coming. Just as you get used to Facebook, you realize the kids see it as so passé, you've embarrassed yourself by even mentioning it. Just as you get used to tapping your card to pay for the shopping, you realize that young people are merely waving their phones at the payment device. Just as you get used to working from home and doing online meetings in a smart shirt or blouse and your pyjama trousers, you hear your job will soon be completely replaced by AI.

Sometimes, no matter how many new tricks you have learned before, you just want it all to stop, so that you can simply get on with the lifestyle you only got used to five minutes ago. In addition, you are getting older, and time seems to be moving faster and faster. It is getting that bit harder to learn each new piece of technology, etiquette or behaviour that is thrown at you.

At a certain point, something gives. Maybe you forget to use the correct pronoun for your grandchild's sexually ambiguous partner. Maybe you find yourself being 'cancelled' for having made a joke about it on Facebook. Maybe you are still referring to an area of your town by the name of a mill that was demolished forty years ago. Maybe you go to a job interview where your potential new boss is half your age and still asking if you have enough 'relevant experience'. Maybe someone laughs at the fact that your solution to any problem with your new smartphone is to randomly stab at buttons and icons until you inadvertently lock it and need to find a young person to fix it for you.

Whatever the flashpoint might be, you find yourself staring up at the heavens and asking, 'What the hell is wrong with this world?' Then you look in the mirror and see a confused, frustrated old person who is as mad as hell and can't take it any more.

So don't tell us we can't learn any new tricks, when we've already learned more than any generation before us ever had to. Instead, maybe try to have a bit of patience when we finally hit that brick wall and turn into exactly the sort of grumpy old bore we always swore we wouldn't be. And feel free to laugh at us as we start to flounder and stumble through the bewildering, brave new world we have somehow found ourselves living in.

The Warning Signs

'Here comes forty. I'm feeling my age and I've ordered the Ferrari. I'm going to get the whole mid-life crisis package.'

KEANU REEVES

For some of us, age brings a welcome excuse for the idiocy we've been prone to for years. For others, 'senior moments' are an entirely new experience. It's all too easy for minor details to slip from busy minds, as former Python and legendary film-maker Terry Gilliam is happy to admit. 'I brush my teeth and then ten minutes later I go back and have to feel the toothbrush. Is it wet? Did I just brush them?'

Are you old before your time?

Bear in mind that the range of indications that you're getting old is now accelerating rapidly. The character Sophia Petrillo once came up with a couple of indicators for impending demise in the American comedy *The Golden Girls*, which she listed, 'One: your children start visiting during the week. Two: your doctor won't let you postdate a cheque.' Today, the mere idea of writing a cheque makes it very clear this is a long way in the past ... And the fact that you are old enough to remember *The Golden Girls* is probably damning enough in the first place.

Perhaps it's time to take stock. Just how close are you to premature maturity? Take a deep breath and let this cautionary checklist help you to figure out whether you are old before your time.

- Waitresses have started to call you 'sweetie'
- You find yourself caring that the neighbour's kids play on your lawn
- All your luggage is on wheels
- You get twitchy when anyone puts their coffee mug down on the table without a coaster
- You not only own a set of coasters, but you also own a set of fine bone china mugs you bought to match the coasters
- You turn down the offer of a night out on the basis that you've been out once already this weekend
- You wake with that 'morning after' feeling and all you did was stay up to paint the living room
- Saturday nights are less about clubbing and more about *Strictly Come Dancing*

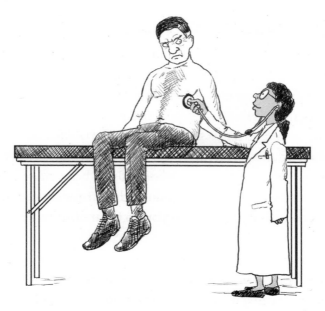

- At hospital appointments, when an apparently pubescent medic starts examining you, you wonder aloud where the 'real' doctor is
- You make that spontaneous 'old person noise' every time you get out of a chair
- Your wardrobe's so outdated it's almost vintage
- You care about your lawn

Embrace your mid-life crisis

Anyone who's recently passed a milestone birthday and immediately fled, panic-stricken, to the nearest Bikram yoga centre, knows the horror that sets in when you first realize you are officially Middle-Aged. For a while, you kid yourself that the advance of time is nothing; your Spotify account, salsa lessons and that glorious set of reflective Lycra cycling gear stand proudly blocking its path. You're only as old as you feel, and you feel great.

Great, that is, until the day your son or daughter sneers at your Spotify playlists, gags at the sight of you and your partner gyrating to Radio 1 in the kitchen, or leaves you for dust when you're out for a jog. Bleakly, you realize you can't fool yourself forever: face it, a nice set of carpet slippers is starting to seem an alluring indoor footwear option and you can't think why you haven't always used a coaster under your drink. You can't even drown your sorrows like you used to: it takes you three days to get over the hangover. Whichever way you swing it, middle age has arrived.

The first thing to do is to get the mid-life crisis over with. Go ahead and get your navel pierced, tattoo that flabby bicep, renew your gym membership or make a move on the office hottie. Whatever floats your boat – just get over it. And then, when you're left wondering what all the fuss was about, take a little time to decide what happens next. How is the rest of your life going to pan out?

What are the options? Are you going to get yourself the best shed on the block and cultivate a passion for home-grown broccoli? Start painting with watercolours, take up membership of a wine club or look forward to an annual cruise?

Or is this all too soon? Well, the good news is that it doesn't have to be that way. These days, middle age brings with it freedoms worth celebrating. You've got the clarity to know what you want and the experience to know how to get it. Gone are the days of gorging on a late-night kebab in the pouring rain, while standing in line for the night bus home. No longer will you be expected to look ripped in your trunks or buff in your bikini, pitch a tent at a rock festival or devote all your free time to maintaining your *Call of Duty* kill rate.

Comfort-wear is where it's at and you can finally admit to yourself that rock festivals always made you tired and irritable. And dirty. It's time to embrace your age-related wisdom; what's more, now you get to lord it up over the younger generation. Who cares if you're irritating, embarrassing or a bore? You've earned the right to tell it like it is and you no longer need to settle for anything less than precisely what you want.

And, hey, if it all goes wrong, you can always blame it on 'the youth of today'. What have you got to lose?

'I'm secretly hoping it's a mid-life crisis,
meaning you're halfway to an early death.'
SUE/JANE LYNCH IN *GLEE*

Keeping it brief

US comedian Steve Cody is a self-titled 'mid-life crisis comic'. He has all the classic signs of mid-life crisis: silver hair, a vigorous interest in mountain climbing and marathon running, and a shiny BMW M3. And, as he likes to share this with his audiences, he has a growing intolerance of the overuse of small talk; an overwhelming impatience for those who are incapable of answering the question, 'How's it going?' with a single word, 'Fine.' Like his friend, Greg, for example. 'Greg never says fine,' complained Steve. 'Instead I get, "Oh, Steve. I just got back from the doctor. My HDL level's too high, my LDL level's too low. Wait till you hear about my colonoscopy report." I know so much about Greg.'

You know those old folks who would always give you a full breakdown on their latest symptoms and health woes when you were waiting for a bus with them. Ask yourself, honestly, is that what you want to turn into?

Time for that mid-life crisis

The past can be a difficult country, darkened by the uncomfortable realization that back then, when you thought you were witty, cool and on-trend, you were actually a pain in the arse. The trouble is, having identified this self-delusion of youth, mid-life can bring with it the painful possibility that nothing has changed.

You're ready for a mid-life crisis if ...

- You can name every member of the current Cabinet
- You can only give your age these days if you do a quick mental calculation
- You have no trouble unfolding a broadsheet newspaper in a cramped space
- You always carry tissues and an umbrella, just in case
- You've finally started flossing
- A night out with your mates rarely involves more than two or three rounds, never ends in a curry and sees you home in time for the *Ten O'Clock News*
- You're frequently incensed by the poor grammar of waiters and shop assistants
- You regularly get your kids' names confused
- Your bathroom cabinet used to be stocked with a year's supply of condoms and Alka-Seltzer. These days, it's where you keep the cod liver oil capsules
- Fashion looks suspiciously like those photos you have of your uni days

If you're just either side of forty, statistically you are more likely to be in the throes of a mid-life crisis now than at any other time. The decade beginning in your mid-thirties is loaded with stress. If you're not careful, long working hours, economic pressures, family responsibilities and the mounting physical signs of middle age conspire to send you into an emotional tailspin. But if you've escaped unscathed so far, perhaps now is the ideal time to start preparing yourself. The mid-life crisis may have been worked to death by comedians and sitcom scriptwriters, but once you have one of your own, you'll know it's no joke.

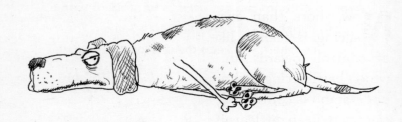

Geeks Run the
World Now

*'Be nice to nerds. Chances are you'll
end up working for one.'*

BILL GATES

Now, more than ever, one of the symptoms of
ageing is feeling like the world is running out
of control towards an incomprehensible future in
which bewildering technology that only young people
understand is controlling every aspect of our lives. We
can try to keep up, learning each new bit of tech that is
thrown at us, but as anyone who ever learned to use a
Blackberry, AOL or Netscape will know, today's shiny
new thing is tomorrow's dinosaur.

Did you know the Flash Player is officially dead? Did
you even know it was alive in the first place?

We might as well give in, accept that the geeks are in
charge, and at least try to understand their psychobabble.

Geek or nerd?

The youth lexicon seems to mutate every couple of months, and keeping up with it can be daunting. Take, for instance, those who are, shall we say, stylishly challenged: are the terms 'geek' and 'nerd' interchangeable, or do they apply to entirely different categories? American comedian Jacob Sirof thinks he has the answer, and is comfortable to label himself a geek, although he adamantly refuses to accept that he's a nerd.

'A geek is the kind of person that'll stand in line to see the midnight premiere of the new Harry Potter movie. That's me, that's how I roll ...' he explains. 'Now a nerd is the kind of person who goes to the midnight premiere of the new Harry Potter movie dressed like Harry Potter. And that shit is pathetic, right? What's up with those losers?'

Thanks for clearing that up, Jacob.

Tron and The Wizard of Oz *were formative for me, so being able to be a part of things like* Tron, Twilight *and* Underworld, *it's much closer to where my heart lies. I'm a nerdy geek.'*

MICHAEL SHEEN

Apps

So how exactly are the new generation of geeks making the world better? Let's take a closer look at modern technology.

You have a lot of apps. Apps for recipes, apps for your bank, apps to play games, apps to read books and newspapers.

As of 2023, there were well over 3.5 million apps available via the Google Play store and, by the look of your monthly bank statement, you have downloaded most of them. Periodically you scroll through pages and pages of these things on your phone and start to wonder what they all do. You can remember being tremendously excited as you downloaded the app on the recommendation of a friend, whose friend was equally enthusiastic when they demonstrated how invaluable it was. It is true that you can pop open an app to see when the next bus is coming, or to navigate a 3D image of the Louvre, or to find out what's going on at NASA but – if you're honest – the need has never arisen.

Perhaps an old dog doesn't need every new trick, after all?

The Internet of things?

Wi-Fi has allowed every gadget in your home to talk to every other gadget. The result is a technological landscape in which you wouldn't dream of buying a toaster unless you could also order books from Amazon on it. This used to be called the 'Internet of things' but now it's the 'metaverse', which basically means your next fridge will nag you if you eat too much fatty food, and your heating control system will give you lectures about global warming if you try to turn it on.

How geeky are you?

- Are you more interested in a movie's special effects than its plot lines?
- Do you, nevertheless, still memorize whole sections of movie dialogue the same way you used to when you were twelve?
- Do you own a rack of T-shirts with obscure slogans, such as, 'Alcohol & calculus don't mix. Never drink & derive', or 'Some things man was never meant to know. For everything else, there's Google'?
- Do you cling to your smartphone during an argument because you never know when you may need ready access to the net to prove that Roddenberry named Lieutenant Geordi La Forge (the one with the bionic spectacles from *Star Trek: Next Generation*) after his favourite Trekkie?
- Have you named a child Leia, Luke, Kirk or Leonard?

Note: That last one is actually a trick question, because if you have, you are merely an ageing geek, who is so far behind the times you can't be seen in the rear-view mirror.

Chief among the offenders is your phone. There was a time when phones were safely attached to the wall by a cable or sat on a special table along with the phone book. Now they follow you everywhere. Your phone syncs to the computer, it docks nicely in the top of your CD player, it tells half a dozen programs where you are and you can use it to operate your TV and access your email. If you have a smartphone, you can use it to discover that you've missed your wife's birthday. It is even conspiring with Alexa behind your back, and secretly sending all your bank details to some malware-toting teenage hoodlum in Eastern Europe or China. Oh, and don't forget that ChatGPT is coming to take your job at the same time.

Anyway, above all, don't worry; this is the future so everything is fine.

Linear TV

Did you know linear TV is dying? Do you even know what linear TV is?

Essentially it is the way old people like us used to watch shows, at the time when they were broadcast, having consulted the TV listings first. Now of course they are all downloadable, so can be binge-watched, Netflixed, live-paused and spread out across a hundred different platforms you have to pay for.

Young people don't even use televisions, having

grown up streaming films and TV programmes on phones, tablets, PC, gaming consoles and so on. But people of our generation are still fond of actual televisions, even if we are getting used to being able to catch up or rewind our favourite shows.

Also, have you noticed how easily modern televisions break? It's just another of the joys of planned obsolescence. But sometimes the old TV isn't even broken; on the contrary, it works fine. But a visit to a friend's house where there are flat screens in the kitchen, the bedrooms and something in front of the sofa that looks more like an IMAX cinema, tips the balance in favour of an upgrade.

For a long time, the only thing a new telly had to offer was a minor increase in size. Every three years, you effectively bought the same product but with a screen that was an inch bigger on either side.

This natural expansion was kept in check by the fact that every inch the TV manufacturers added at the sides translated into four inches at the back and about a stone in weight. Unless you lived in a long thin room with a reinforced floor you'd eventually be in trouble.

Then they went flat screen. Without a vast, hot box behind them, TVs could become massive and still leave you with plenty of leg room. Then the eggheads looked for new ways to keep us glued to the box.

So it is that you find yourself in the electrical shop being shown a 3D HD LED 65-inch TV with full Internet access by an enthusiastic middle-aged man with bad breath and a clip-on tie. When combined with four sets of powered 3D glasses, eight surround speakers and a wall-mounting unit, this smart TV is more expensive than a Smart Car. You put it on the credit card, or stick it on Klarna, and arrange for a courier to ship the thing to your home.

Cut to three weeks later. One wall of your living room is taken up by the daunting TV, but you're up in your office watching *The Apprentice* on your tablet. It turns out that the new TV has such disturbing pinpoint clarity that you are frightened to turn it on for fear of having to endure every pore on the lead actor's face. Explosions in surround sound set off the car alarm in the street outside and it uses so much electricity that when you change channels, the street lights dim.

Feeling like an old dog yet?

Syncing gadgets

Ever since the invention of the stacked hi-fi system in the 1970s, geeks have been working to splice every piece of technology together.

In the heady days of the hi-fi stack, this dismal practice was kept in check by practical limitations – notably that the cassette deck had to be no more than a cable's length away from the tuner, which made syncing an exercise in piling things on top of one another. However, the invention of Wi-Fi has meant that the gloves are off.

Keep taking the tablets

Like everyone else in Western society, you are a tech-addicted consumer who believes that buying anything square and shiny with an ominous screen will vastly improve your standing among your friends, make you more efficient at work and generally give a sense of meaning and purpose to the hollow farce that is your life. It might even contribute to educating your kids because God knows you have neither the time nor the inclination to do so.

But one question lingers at the back of your mind as you stride into the store with your credit card held aloft: what does a tablet do?

Is it really a big smartphone? Or is it just a computer without a keyboard? Will your friends laugh at you if it isn't a folding one? Is it for watching films or reading books? It's clearly too big to replace your mobile, yet it's much too small to replace your TV. You can't really type on it, nor can you make phone calls, so it's no good for business. It also doesn't have a joystick or a keypad so it's really no good for games.

While it would clearly be great for chopping vegetables on or as a drinks tray, they never seem to be used for that in the adverts.

Of course, these doubts don't stop you handing over the cash and scuttling home like a squirrel that's burgled a nut factory. When you get home it soon becomes clear that all the tablet is really good for is looking at cool stuff – by which you mean looking at your own house from above on Google Maps. Is that really worth four hundred quid? Of course it is.

The lost art of reading

You love to read so it comes as something of a surprise that you don't do it any more. The only time you buy books in a bookshop is at Christmas and even then it is usually a last-minute purchase for a difficult-to-buy-for nephew.

Determined to get back on the literary ladder, you pay a visit to your local bookshop. Naturally it has closed down and been turned into a coffee shop, so you get back in the car and finally find a bookshop buried in a nearby mall. Stepping across the threshold, you are quite surprised to find that half the shop floor is taken up with gifts, novelty bookmarks, CDs, children's toys and a coffee shop. There are a couple of books at the back so you accept this diversification in retail bookselling as another sign of the times.

As you browse this meagre offering you realize that, despite seeing yourself as a keen reader, most of your discussions about books at dinner parties are based entirely on reviews you read in the Sunday supplement. If you are honest, 90 per cent of your actual reading takes the form of celebrity gossip in free newspapers on the way home from work, recipes and idly flipping through twenty-year-old paperbacks you already own while sitting on the loo. You resolve to rectify this situation immediately by buying a new Kindle.

Read all about it

Superficially, the Kindle is pretty exciting. It comes in a nice box and looks a bit like an iPad. The manufacturer claims it is really easy to search for and download books, and you duly install twenty free classic titles from *Jane Eyre* to *Dracula* that you've always wanted to read but never did. But you soon discover that the Kindle successfully recreates what you didn't like about books in the first instance: they take ages to read. In a time when you can play basic games on the colour display on your fridge, this situation is too boring to be tolerated. Admittedly, you can do some clever things like add bookmarks and make a note on the text but you never did that with real books, so what's the point? To add insult to injury, when you download new digital titles, they're barely any cheaper than the heavily discounted hard copies in the shop.

In the end, rather than saving you money, the Kindle turns out to be a more expensive way to read because, two weeks later, you leave it on the train.

You just can't teach an old dog new tricks.

A droning noise

The chances are that soon your postman and delivery drivers will be redundant, as they will have been replaced by an ungodly combination of driverless cars and drones that carry your parcel to your door. However, as with all new tech, it's worth bearing in mind that these extraordinary unmanned aerial vehicles (UAVs) or drones were initially designed for military purposes.

Remote controllers

Also, the drones are probably being controlled by a group of recently enlisted school-leavers in a giant call centre in Nevada. It will only be a matter of time before some hungover and heartbroken twenty-year-old employs this same technology to provide him with twenty-four-hour surveillance of his ex-girlfriend's house or to incinerate the car of his former headmaster. Only then will we realize that basing our military strategy around a group of pimply youths who have spent the last five years in their bedroom playing *World of Warcraft* may not have been that sensible.

So when you see that drone carrying your latest pointless tech purchase to the door, bear in mind that, if you say one wrong word, it might morph into a flying equivalent of RoboCop, and administer some rough justice to punish you for failing to upgrade to a more expensive shopping scheme.

AI

The latest bit of genius from the geeks is the rapid rollout of AI. ChatGPT, along with Midjourney and the latest generation of music generators, mean that anyone can come up with text, images and songs without having to pay someone to do it. This means that the jobs of everyone from lawyers to medics to media hacks are imminently under threat. Great.

The technology experts assure us that every tech breakthrough that costs some people their jobs also leads to new job opportunities, so there is no problem. But who do you think they are going to choose to employ as a service assistant maintaining the functioning of our robot overlords: you or a twenty-something who learned to read using a mobile phone?

This is one tech advance that may be doomed to fail sooner than expected: already, when generative AIs scrape the web, they are feeding on (and effectively stealing) not only centuries of human endeavour, but also each other's efforts, meaning the outputs are becoming more and more scrambled and meaningless.

Now the geeks are frantically warning each other that AI could destroy the world as we know it and suggesting that maybe we should slow down until we understand what hell they are unleashing on us all. Will anyone listen?

What are the odds? There is serious money to be made here. But maybe we old dogs did know the best tricks, after all?

The Inevitability of Decrepitude

*'Have you not a moist eye, a dry hand, a
yellow cheek, a white beard, a decreasing leg,
an increasing belly? Is not your voice broken,
your wind short, your chin double, your
wit single, and every part about
blasted with antiquity?'*

WILLIAM SHAKESPEARE,
HENRY IV, PART II

Are you beginning to curse Isaac Newton and his godawful theories about gravity every time you catch a glimpse of yourself naked? The uncomfortable truth is that as the ravaging effects of your days of sex, drugs and rock 'n' roll make themselves ever more apparent, you are fast approaching the most painful dilemma of the recently past-it. How to proceed from here needs careful consideration.

Let's look at your options:

- Embrace the Church of Spanx, and invest in gravity-defying underwear that will prop up your sagging chest and strap down your flabby midriff
- Prostrate yourself under the surgeon's knife, allowing yourself to be sliced, pumped and remodelled into better shape
- Worship at the altar of Madonna, embracing yoga and a raw food diet while adopting a brood of infants to keep you on your toes

If you are beginning to empathize with the late actor Richard Harris, who once said, 'My face is like five miles of bad country road,' don't despair. Perhaps there's another way. Be true to who you are, vow to age disgracefully and throw a finger to the convention that only young is beautiful! As Billy Connolly says, 'Fuck handsome ... rich works!'

'My husband said, "Show me your boobs," and I had to pull up my skirt ... so it was time to get them done!'

DOLLY PARTON

Letting it all hang out

Many of our more 'mature' celebrities show no sign of hiding their bodies away and perhaps none more so than the indefatigable Bette Midler. Bette used to be known to bare a boob or two mid-concert and she is candid about a peculiar preoccupation she has with her breasts: she likes to know how much they weigh. 'Got myself a little mail scale, the kind they weigh postage and cocaine on. Unhooked my bra, flopped one of those suckers down ... I won't tell ya how much they weigh but it costs $87.50 to send 'em to Brazil ... third class!'

Toilet breaks

The author John Mortimer certainly knew all about the trials and tribulations of growing old, for as he once said, 'When you get to my age, life seems little more than one long march to and from the lavatory.'

Letting yourself go

Women definitely know they are in the late flush of youth when they spend more and more hours each week at the beauty salon, trying to stave off old age.

For example, the American novelist and screenwriter Nora Ephron wrote: 'I am only about eight hours a week away from looking like a bag lady, with the frizzled, flyaway grey hair I would probably have if I stopped dying mine; with a pot belly I would definitely develop if I ate just half of what I think about eating every day; with the dirty nails and chapped lips and moustache and bushy eyebrows that would be my destiny if I ever spent two weeks on a desert island.'

Exercise is bad for you

Exercise can be very bad for you at any age, but the older you get, the worse it can become. Australian author Clive James knew this only too well:

'Joggers are people who really believe that they can recapture their youth by taking exercise. The brutal facts suggest that unless you have never lost your youth, and have been taking exercise all the time, then trying to get fit will kill you as surely as a horse-kick to the heart.'

The dreaded menopause

Women sometimes get to know they're 'not as young as they were' when their bodies begin giving out increasingly desperate signals – otherwise known as the menopause. Here are a few ways to discover if you are experiencing 'oestrogen issues':

- Everyone around you has an attitude problem
- You're adding chocolate flakes to your savoury pie
- The dryer has shrunk every last pair of your trousers
- Your husband is suddenly agreeing with everything you say
- You're using your mobile phone to dial up every bumper sticker that says: 'How's my driving? Call 0207 ...'

Hair today ...

If the menopause is a sign that women are getting older, surely it follows that baldness is a sign that men aren't quite the youthful creatures they used to be.

Being 'follically challenged' is something that the eminent British philosopher Thomas Hobbes knew all about. In his eighties, Hobbes was almost completely bald, but he wouldn't wear a hat, claiming he never suffered from head colds.

Instead, the biggest problem 'was to keep flies from pitching on the baldness'.

... Gone tomorrow

Or how about this observation from US comic writer Dave Barry on how those men who try to cover up their baldness only show themselves to be more past it than most?

'The method preferred by most balding men for making themselves look silly is called the "comb-over", which is when the man grows the hair on one side of his head very long and combs it across the bald area, creating an effect that looks from the top like an egg in the grasp of a large tropical spider.'

> *'My grandma told me, "The good news is, after menopause the hair on your legs gets really thin and you don't have to shave any more. Which is great because it means you have more time to work on your new moustache."'*

KAREN HABER

Sorry for your loss

A receding hairline in your late twenties can get you down. An expanding bald patch in your late thirties is depressing. By your forties, it's possible we're not talking 'hair' so much as 'hairs'. The trouble is that just as you come to terms with your current state of hair loss, you can be sure that an all-new stage is waiting just around the corner. And coaxing you into parting with your hard-earned cash to combat your moulting is, of course, a multibillion-dollar global industry. So in case you're ever tempted to splash out on largely ineffectual, artificial anti-hair-loss treatments, pay an uplifting visit to baldrus.com, a website devoted to high-fiving the hairless, and urging men everywhere to 'just say no to rugs, drugs, plugs ... and comb-overs'.

> 'The thing you notice here after America is how refreshingly ordinary people look because they haven't had their chin wrapped around the back of their ears.'
>
> SIR IAN MCKELLEN

Sofa surfing

In a rare moment of self-awareness you realize that you're unlikely to get off the sofa without prompting. You can't afford a personal trainer so you invest in an activity tracker, whether it be a Fitbit or any of a plethora of similar systems. Thus equipped, you can enjoy runs in which the music in your headphones is constantly interrupted by a disturbingly upbeat voice counting down the kilometres (you can't work out how to switch it to miles), until you hit your goal – usually the newsagents at the end of the street. While this disembodied encouragement is undoubtedly motivating as you jog confidently out of the house, it starts to grate when you are bent double, pouring sweat and fighting for breath half a mile later.

Even worse, you have foolishly chosen to connect

your tracker to your Facebook page in the belief that this will somehow keep you on track. This means that the distance of your runs and the time it has taken you are now posted online; so your friends can follow your enthusiastic first attempts then watch you get slower and slower over shorter distances, before finally stopping all together.

Is this a new trick you don't need to learn?

An entirely new relationship with breasts

Lots of men will identify with the trials and tribulations of middle-aged writer and journalist Stephen J. Lyons, who has been open about his ongoing battle with his ageing body. His altered experience of the locker room will be familiar enough to most mid-life men: gone are

the days when you could gambol naked and proud, playing whiplash by snapping your towel. Writing on the website salon.com, he complained: 'Showers are not for lingering any more, nor can I comfortably flex and strut in front of a mirror. Instead, when I sneak a peek at my reflection, I notice ... a disturbing jiggling motion around the chest area. Breasts! When I bend over, cleavage! Although most men adore breasts, they do not want their own pair ...'

Cosmetic consumerism

You like to think that you're pretty content with the way you look, even though you've always held a grudging respect for those who are prepared to go under the knife to achieve a straight nose, or a smooth jaw. You like to think that you are not so vain that you would feel the need to have surgery and ignore the fact that you lack the necessary courage to take the plunge anyway. Instead you choose to plough a considerable amount of your time and a hefty proportion of your disposable income into any product that promises radical improvements to your looks without recourse to a stay in a private clinic.

This goes a long way to explain why you can't shut your bathroom cupboard for bottles of fake tan, facial rehydration lotion and skin-firming gel. You know these potions are no better for you than rubbing lard on your skin on a hot day. But you're a sucker for anything that smells of aloe vera and is advertised by either a rugged man rubbing his unshaven chin or a youthful-looking, recently showered woman displaying her glowing hair for all to see, particularly if there is a pseudo-scientific explanation to go with it.

But just how far can you go to look good without being vain? Is having your teeth whitened or electrolysis on your hairy bits as bad as Botox? And does having laser eye surgery or unflattering braces on your teeth count as plastic surgery or a commitment to long-term health?

Before you lose too much sleep over this, it might be worth considering the fact that it doesn't really matter if you have smooth, tanned skin and a dazzling smile, when your paunch is hanging over the top of your designer jeans like your bottom half has melted.

'The media would have us believe that ageing
is harder for women, which might be true,
but then, hey, men age too. For example,
how hairy are my toes becoming?'

JEFF GREEN

'*You go to the gym, right, and they got a machine for every body part. You know – they got something for the legs, the arms, the back. But you know, you can't walk up to the trainer and be like, "Where's the man-tit machine at?"*'

TODD LYNN

Hugh's brief encounter

Let's face it, the physical discomforts of middle age can be unpleasant – and to add insult to injury, there's a whole new world of invasive medical check-ups waiting just around the corner. Billy Connolly sums it up nicely: 'See, there's a terrible thing that happens to men after fifty: your doctor loses all interest in your testicles, and takes an overwhelming interest in your arsehole.'

Hugh Grant is no stranger to embarrassment; let's face it, he has a history of being discovered in compromising positions. But I digress. A few years ago, he was horrified to discover during a long train journey that he had been struck with one of the ugly secrets of middle age: haemorrhoids.

'I felt something strange in my buttocks. As I had never had haemorrhoids, I did not understand what was happening,' he confessed in a magazine interview. He decided to head to the toilet to investigate further. 'But it was damn hard, because it was a small toilet. I finished up standing on the bezel ... [trying to bend and] twist myself to see myself in the mirror. But, like a fool, I forgot to lock the door. And when I had my buttocks wide open, a woman entered the toilet and found herself nose to nose with the most intimate part of my anatomy ...'

> 'I feel very, very old. My hair hurts. I have
> buttocks all over my body and I can't even
> smoke properly any more. I don't have lungs;
> I just have two poppadoms in here.'

DYLAN MORAN

Time to dye?

As soon as your hair starts going grey, it's an undeniable sign that your best years are behind you. Billy Connolly observed, 'I'm so grey, I look like I'm going to rain sometimes.'

It starts with the odd grey hair, quickly pulled out in horror, then it spreads across your temples and before you know it you're at the pharmacy asking for DIY hair dye labelled Autumn Chestnut. There's no question that greying hair is ageing. But less commonly discussed is whether there is a need to colour greying hair in less visible areas ... One episode of *Sex in the City* addressed this very issue when man-eater Samantha was horrified to discover a single grey pubic hair. Deciding to colour her way out of the situation, Sam then left the colour treatment on for too long, resulting in flaming red pubes.

> *'I found my first grey pubic hair the other*
> *day. It was in a kebab, but there you go.'*
>
> JEFF GREEN

Men care about ageing too

As we all know, the anti-ageing industry isn't just big bucks for a female market. As US comedian Greg Fitzsimmons says, male ageing is a big business too, just take a look at the big money-spinners in the pharmaceutical industry. 'These are the big breakthroughs in science and technology in the last ten years: we have Rogaine, Prozac ... Viagra. You get a sense for who's bankrolling medical research in this country. It's just depressed, balding, white guys who can't get erections any more.'

Sporting injuries

A curious consequence of the ageing process is a subtle change in how you spend your free time. In your younger days, downtime was all about long nights in the pub followed by drunken karaoke. Weekend rock festivals,

midweek comedy gigs and the odd house party was where it was at.

But soon enough, career, family and responsibility make an evil pact to ensure that you simply don't have the stamina for too much late-night fun. Weekends are set aside for an entirely new range of leisure pursuits, many of which are a reaction to the onset of Middle-Aged Spread. Open your wardrobe and there's a good chance there'll be Lycra lurking in there somewhere. Perhaps you've got a racing bike, suspended from the garage wall. Or even (God forbid) a wetsuit, in case you are mad enough ever to go windsurfing again.

Anything but exercise!

However much we might hate it, there comes a time when a guy has to man up to the need to get in shape.

The excess booze, the cigarettes and the fast-food diet have to go once you get to a certain age. And if you indulged in all those bad habits, it can be tough trying to tackle them all at once.

US comedian Gene Pompa knows exactly how tough. 'I quit smoking cigarettes about a year ago,' he told an audience. 'I gained eighteen pounds. So now I have to wear a lot of black so no one knows what a big hunk of pig I turned into. No matter what I do, I cannot lose this eighteen pounds. It's really starting to kick my ass. I mean I have tried everything short of diet and exercise.'

> *'I'm not interested in any of these recreational activities where, you know, I'm trying to have fun and yet not die at the same time.'*
>
> **JOHNNY LAMPERT**

How to lose the love handles

If you've gained a few pounds here and there over the years, stepping up the fitness regime should help you shift them. But if you've gained a few pounds everywhere, there's no avoiding it: you're going to have to diet. And choosing the right diet for you can be tricky.

US comedian J. Anthony Brown happened upon the perfect diet for him after reading an interview with the late great Barry White: 'He said what he did was take all of his clothes off, and he stood naked in front of the mirror. I said, "That's a damn good diet." I think I could lose weight, too, if I saw Barry White naked, huh? Like, "You hungry?" "No man, I just saw Barry White naked. I don't want nothing."'

The long pursuit of the perfect gym body

Some bodies are just not meant for muscle – and if you've not learned that by now, maybe it's time you got real. Comedian Mike Birbiglia has learned the hard way.

'I try and go to the gym. But it seems kind of counterproductive because the idea is to impress women, but there are women at the gym and they can see me bench-pressing sixty-five pounds. And I don't think they're saying, "Check out the guy in the dress socks. I saw him do one chin-up and then fall on the ground."'

The Inevitability of Decrepitude

'What do you do – eat the right foods, exercise?
Live till you're ninety-seven so your relatives
can empty your urine bottle every five minutes?
Oh, thanks for living so long, Grandpa. All I
want to do is tend to your bodily fluids!'

JOEY KOLA

Exactly how active is active?

It's old news that we in the West are getting fatter and lazier. Mechanization, easy transport and sedentary lifestyles along with fast food and bad diets are dooming us to obesity. We know that already. We also know we need to take personal responsibility to sort ourselves and our children out. But periodically it falls on public and government-sponsored agencies to try to establish quite how bad the situation is.

A few years back, America's Centers for Disease Control and Prevention decided to take a survey into American lifestyles, the second such survey it had

undertaken. This time, to get a more comprehensive picture of exactly how active the American nation was, the CDC decided to loosen its definition of 'activity'. Moderate exercise had been defined in earlier surveys: gardening, walking, housework, ballroom dancing and so on. This time, they decided to ask Americans about the extent of their indulgence in 'light activity', including fishing, sitting down, shooting a pistol, photocopying, playing darts or pool, colouring-in, taking a whirlpool bath and even 'purposeless wandering'. Even with these generous allowances, the CDC concluded bleakly that Americans just aren't active enough.

It's not just the old dogs ...

Musical Chairs

*'I'd rather be dead than singing
"Satisfaction" when I'm forty-five.'*

MICK JAGGER

Nothing dates you more instantly than your musical tastes. Sometime between the age of thirty and forty, a switch goes in your brain, and suddenly you lose all interest in listening to anything you haven't heard a thousand times before. In one respect, this is logical: the older generation largely defined themselves in tribal terms; you were a goth, a mod, an indie kid, a punk, a prog rock fan, a Northern Rocker, a sixties geek or whatever. Modern youths have a very different mindset, as they have Spotify and can access any music they want. They don't identify themselves through their music, as they mostly have deeply eclectic tastes, but through which Internet forum or social media platform they prefer to advertise themselves on, or which games they play.

So you reach an age where your brain is too full of old songs to load any new ones, and there you are: stuck, unless you make a heroic effort to listen to the songs your kids or grandkids are playing, in which case your only reward will be derision when you point out it sounds a bit like Kate Bush or Bob Dylan.

Meanwhile, we have seen a succession of our icons dying of old age, sometimes when they were younger than we are ourselves. It's like a game of musical chairs, in which we constantly ask ourselves, 'How is it possible that David Bowie/Sinead O' Connor/Terry Hall/Aretha Franklin is dead but_____/_____/_____ is still alive?' (You can fill in the blanks with your own least favourite living musicians; we are trying to be kind here. Also, I don't want to be dragged up in court for a libel case.)

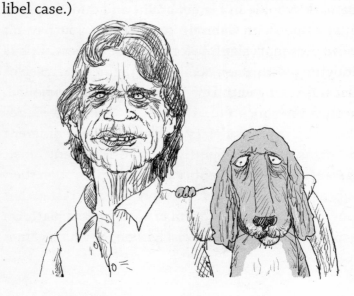

Mick Jagger is a bellwether here. Some might call him another word with the prefix bell-, but, as I said, we're trying to be kind here. His youthful desire not to age disgracefully has come to nought; at the age of eighty he was planning to go back out on the road, promoting the latest Rolling Stones' album.

See, old dogs can at least repeat old tricks, even if they said they wouldn't.

A fate worse than death?

The great jazz musician Louis Armstrong had a love of life and a passion for what he did that was inspirational. He is also to be admired for his straight-talking attitude towards death. He once said, with that trademark twinkle in his eye, 'When I go to the Gate, I'll play a duet with Gabriel.' But after the death of his beloved personal valet Doc Pugh, when asked what had been wrong with Pugh, Louis replied philosophically, 'What was wrong with Doc? When you die, everything is wrong with you.'

Not so cool

Hip-hop rapper and actor LL Cool J was once asked in an interview if he still expected to be rapping in thirty years' time. 'We'll see what Vegas is paying,' he said. 'I'll be rapping about denture cream, Preparation H. My pants will still be sagging – but it'll be from Depends [incontinence pads]!'

> 'When I'm playing Rock Band, I'm like, "Man, someday, later on in life when I'm a famous rock star ..." Which gets a little harder to convince myself of as I reach middle age, but it still happens a lot.'
>
> TIM SCHAFER

The rock star life

In January 2003, rock groups KISS and Aerosmith announced that they were going to embark on their first world tour together during the forthcoming summer. 'They could call it the Tongue and Lips Tour,' *Salon*'s Amy Reiter suggested.

Sometime later, it was pointed out that the groups had played together more than thirty years earlier.'On the other hand,' Reiter then joked, 'maybe they should call it the Dentures and Bifocals Tour.'

The Rock-Bottom Remainders

By the time you've hit true maturity, if all's gone according to plan, you should be enjoying some prowess at your chosen trade. You've worked long and hard to hone your skills and you've built a solid reputation in the process. Of course, there will always be those who reach the top rung only to discover they've been climbing the wrong ladder all along. These are the types who harbour a deep-seated hankering for something entirely different, which no amount of success can quash.

Take, for instance some of most successful living writers: Amy Tan, Steven King, Matt Groening, Ridley Pearson and Dave Barry. Their work is recognized the world over and has ensured that they can look forward to living out their days in comfort. But they discovered they had common ground beyond their ability to write: none of them had ever shaken off a desire to be in a rock band. It didn't take long for 'The Rock-Bottom Remainders' to be born.

The self-professed 'really bad' rock musicians were soon hailed by critics as having 'one of the world's highest ratios of noise to talent'. No surprise, given that they pay little attention to rehearsal or planning and a great deal more to general high-jinks and where to go for their slap-up, post-gig dinner. They decided that at their stage in life, all that matters is having fun on their own terms.

So, sometimes you *can* teach old dogs a new trick – they just might not be very good at it …

The Rock-Bottom Remainders are also entirely sanguine about their small and idiosyncratic band of loyal followers. 'What I have found,' said Dave Barry, 'is that our groupies are ageing librarians and, even at my advanced age, I can outrun them pretty easily.'

'I'm sad. I'm officially a sad fifty-five-year-old.'

DAMON ALBARN, 2023

An indecorous way to go

One way to try to pretend you're still young is to go under the surgeon's knife. But you're taking a huge leap of faith that they will act safely, ethically and as you have requested. We've all heard the horror stories about when cosmetic surgery goes horribly wrong. And every once in a while, a procedure turns out to be deadly.

Hugh Massingberd, a former editor of the obituaries page of the *Daily Telegraph*, recalled in an article for *The Spectator*, how he had once been instructed by the editor of the *Telegraph* to include a cause of death in every obit. Massingberd felt this to be an unseemly requirement, which he demonstrated the following day by running an obit for an American jazz player who had, as he put it, 'handed in his dinner pail after a penile implant had unfortunately exploded'. Massingberd having proved his point, the editor capitulated.

As for the jazz player: well, isn't that a story that will make you count your blessings (in inches)?

The dork side

If you think you're too entrenched in your geeky ways to do anything about it, allow yourself to be inspired by a punk rock legend. Bryan 'Dexter' Holland, of American rock band The Offspring, has been hailed as 'one of the greatest punk vocalists in rock history' (according to the website IMDb), as well as being credited with bringing punk to middle-class, suburban America. But the wild man of American punk wasn't ever particularly feral. 'Dexter' was valedictorian of his high school in a wealthy Californian suburb and has a Master's degree in molecular biology. If he can make the leap, so can you.

Feel the pain

During an appearance on Conan O'Brien's TV show, American comedian Tracy Morgan revealed how all of his friends were trying to become rap artists, including his forty-one-year-old brother.

'What's he rapping about?' Conan joked. 'Lower back pain?'

Time for reinvention

On the subject of our tastes as twenty-somethings, that tribal stage of musical tastes was also reflected in our sartorial choices. Do you ever look at twenty-somethings and wonder if they know how absurd they look? And then do you have that chilling moment when you realize that's exactly what everyone over forty thought about your younger self's fashion choices? This is followed by the equally chilling realization that you now dress pretty much exactly like your parents and grandparents did thirty years ago: maybe not the exact same clothing, but the same inflexible rigidity when it comes to trying something new, or changing your hairstyle.

Let's assume you've reached the life stage where your own 'adulthood' is no longer deniable. That 'certain age' when suddenly everyone you know has become rather staid and conventional? Do sober dinner parties and smug barbecues on decked terraces threaten to clog up your weekends? Is the conversation around you a relentless cycle of Sancerre and house prices? Are you beginning to wonder whether there is, in fact, life beyond middle age?

If so, it's high time you rebel, and not just by dressing for dinner in ripped jeans and battered Doc Martens. Maybe try to learn a new trick.

Finding middle-age cool

Reinventing yourself can be as simple as discovering an all-new middle-aged cool. There are plenty of role models out there, so for inspiration you need do nothing more than keep your eyes peeled. As US comedian Demetri Martin discovered, a little observation can go a long way when it comes to figuring out a working definition of 'cool': 'I was at a party the other night, and I saw a guy wearing a leather jacket, and I thought, "That is cool." Like, ten minutes later, I saw a guy wearing a leather vest and I thought, "That is not cool." That's when I realized cool is all about leather sleeves.'

You know you're an old dog when ...

- You look forward to a dull evening at home
- You finally got your head together – and now your body is disintegrating
- Getting lucky means you find your car in the parking lot
- Your worst enemy is gravity
- You talk about good grass and you're discussing someone's lawn
- You have a party and your neighbours don't even realize
- You receive more get-well cards than bills
- People call at 9 p.m. and ask, 'Did I wake you?'
- You know what the word 'equity' means
- Your TV is as loud as it can get and you still can't hear it
- You find yourself beginning to like folk music
- You no longer reach for the moon. In fact, you have difficulty reaching for your toes

Middle-aged geek chic

As we may have mentioned, there's a degree of kudos these days to being a nerd. 'Geek chic' has been perpetuated by TV sitcoms such as *The Big Bang Theory* and *Glee*. It's now cool to be uncool – but don't be fooled, it's a rule that only works below a certain age. The closer you get to middle age, the more you tread perilous ground if you admit to a working understanding of binary maths or an ability to swear in Klingon.

Some of you may already be entirely settled in the world of the geek – far too comfortable with your leather elbow-patch sweaters and your box set of *Battlestar Galactica*. For the rest of you, there may still be some hope.

Old Dogs and
the Drink

*'I hate middle age. Too young for the
bowling green, too old for Ecstasy.'*
GREGOR FISHER, IN *RAB C. NESBITT*

Sooner or later we all have to face up to the fact that the days of partying till dawn and still making it into work the next morning are over. These days, a night on the sauce on a Saturday can leave you still feeling jaded on Monday morning. It's time to learn to pace yourself. Know your own limits. Comedian Micky Flanagan admitted recently, 'I can't do this partying any more ... I've reached the point where if I queue for a nightclub and the bouncer says, "You can come in," I say, "Thanks, mate ... my feet are killing me."'

What's your poison?

Even for bright young things in their twenties, there's nothing like a hangover to give you a taste of what it's like to be 107 years old. And yet few of us ever entirely free ourselves from the lure of our favourite vice – whether that's a cold beer, a cool Chardonnay, a fresh pack of cigarettes or simply hot, strong coffee in plentiful supply. Oh yeah, we make empty pledges periodically, promising ourselves we'll either cut back or cut out but, as Humphrey Bogart once said, 'I gave up drinking once – it was the worst afternoon of my entire life.'

However, it's not all bad news. Studies confirm that not only is red wine a useful tool in the fight against heart disease, but it also has a positive effect at slowing the ageing of the eyes, as well as helping stave off cataracts. Of course, that nasty word 'moderation' cannot be overlooked, but pour yourself a restrained glass or two, and settle back to enjoy these tales of the overindulgence of others – particularly elders who should have known better.

Blind drunk

'One drink is just right; two is too many; three is too few.' So warns a Danish drinking proverb, as well it might to the nation with the most ready access to alcohol of any Scandinavian country.

Danish-born writer and broadcaster Sandi Toksvig is well known for her intoxicating ability to spin a colourful yarn or two. As she revealed on an episode of the television quiz show *QI*, her Danish grandfather happily shared the national predilection for a tipple. At some point in his life he had lost an eye.

'But he wasn't careless,' Sandi explained, 'he was ill.' He had had the eye replaced with an ice-blue glass eye, a perfect match to his good Scandinavian-blue one. But he didn't stop at just the one glass eye. 'He had [another] one made that was bloodshot. It was known as "Grandpa's Party Eye", and he kept it in a box on the mantelpiece.

'And when he was going out, he would take out the false blue one and put in the bloodshot one. He'd say, "I'm going out now and I shan't be back till they match!"'

'Sometimes getting older feels easy; sometimes it feels difficult. It depends how the wine is hitting you really.'

RUPERT EVERETT

Drink till you're seeing stars

No matter how old they get, some guys will still go to any lengths for a free pint. From statesmen to barmen, rocket scientists to motor mechanics, some guys never turn down a beer. *The New York Times* reported the findings of Dr Tom Millar, a silver-haired astrophysicist from the University of Manchester. Dr Millar was one of a team of British scientists who succeeded in analysing an interstellar gas cloud a thousand times bigger than our solar system, and discovered that it contains enough alcohol to make an eye-watering 400 trillion trillion pints of beer. So perhaps from now on, astrophysicists will never die, they'll head straight to that great bierkeller in the sky.

'Young guys go chasing women every night. You do that, you're called party animals. Do that in middle age, you're called a lonely alcoholic.'

MARK CRAIG TAYLOR

Sex, drugs ... and palm trees?

It sounds like a rock 'n' roll myth: a rock guitar legend living the high life in Fiji, with the help of close friends and just a sniff or two of cocaine. Sun, sea, sand and palm trees. Our rock star, feeling invincible after a night of narcotic indulgence, insists on shimmying up a huge palm tree. Seconds later, he plunges out of the tree and lands on his head. It's no myth: it's just one of the many near-death experiences of Rolling Stone Keith Richards, who was clearly not so much invincible as, well, caned.

The fall was a nasty one, necessitating an emergency operation to fit a metal plate in his skull. But if you're imagining this to be a story from Richards's halcyon days in the 1960s, you'd be wrong.

Old Dogs and the Drink

This was 2006, and the man, once dubbed 'The World's Most Elegantly Wasted Human Being', was sixty-three at the time. But, just to prove that it's never too late to turn over a new leaf, the Fiji incident proved to be the final jolt Richards needed. He hasn't taken cocaine since, and has been heroin-free for more than three decades. And, even more amazing, at the time of writing, he's still alive. Perhaps there's hope for us all?

'I stopped drinking the day I couldn't find my way out of a telephone box. I rang my manager in a panic. He told me it couldn't be difficult. "There's only four walls and the phone is on one of them for Christ's sake."'

BILLY CONNOLLY

The Art of
Failing Upwards

*'If you know you are going to
fail, then fail gloriously!'*

CATE BLANCHETT

They used to say that all political careers end in failure. These days it might be simpler to say that all careers end in failure. The world is run by young people, who mostly seem to hold to the theory that, yes, employees over the age of fifty have a lot of experience, but firstly, it's all from the past, which was a foreign country, and secondly, they are more expensive than a teenager, and slightly less immunized to a world of zero hours contracts and the gig economy.

Even if we still have jobs, it is all very different now. The pandemic led to a long-overdue shift to working from home. Wouldn't that have been great in our twenties or thirties? Saving all that time and money

on transport, and having the flexibility to arrange our work around our lives rather than the other way round.

Somehow it hasn't turned out quite like that. Instead we find ourselves muting daytime TV, carefully positioning the laptop to point away from the chaotic mess of our front room, and putting on a shirt over our pants, joggers or pyjama trousers so that we at least look acceptable from the waist up, before stabbing randomly at the icons on a Zoom or Teams call, uncertain which one turns the camera and sound on. Then we have awkward conversations slightly out of sync with our colleagues or clients.

You can't teach an old dog new tricks – and the end result is still going to be redundancy or a kind of stalemate in which we're only hanging onto our jobs to try to top up the pension we started paying into far too late.

So when we run into the wall of failure, what are our options? Knuckle down and try to scrape a living from the gig economy? Move to a country cottage and live off the grid? Take up an exotic new hobby? Finish that godawful novel we never got the time to write?

There are so many options. It's just that none of them sound that great. But here are some examples of old dogs who made a change, with varying results.

All work and no play

We've all come across the career maniac and, let's be honest, there's nothing worse. This is the individual who has lived to work for a couple of decades or more, and now has very little else. The kind of person who generally has no patience to sit through a movie and no inclination to eat in company; in any case, leisure time for them is such a rare thing, they have almost certainly forgotten how to fill it. Their smartphone ranks as their most prized possession and life has become one endless cycle of work, gym and sleep.

If this all sounds horribly familiar, perhaps it's time you did something about it. Walk away from the mobile, take the weekend off and try really relaxing for once.

Live the dream. Period.

Middle-aged single, childless graphic artist Harry Finley
lived what he described as 'a pretty dull life' in a small
town in Maryland. But an interest that was first sparked
when he lived and worked in Europe during the 1980s,
took on a life of its own when Finley decided to turn his
'hobby' into a museum. His collection, the only one of
its kind, attracted international press attention.

So – what is Finley's passion? Not what you might
first imagine of a single male graphic artist. Finley is
curator of the world's only Museum of Menstruation,
an extensive collection of feminine hygiene products
and vintage tampon advertisements from all over the
world. Finley is living proof that so long as you have
the courage to stem the flow of an otherwise average
existence, it's never too late to pursue your dream.

From one circus act to another

A major life change is never easy; it takes a lot of
courage to admit you're not happy – and more to do
something about it. How much harder, then, when
you have a face full of ink and are a professional freak-
show act at Coney Island, lying on a bed of nails for a
living under the name of 'The Pain-Proof Man'. That's
exactly where Eduardo Arrocha had been for more
than a decade. Bored of the daily grind, he yearned for
mental stimulation, and finally made the decision, at

forty-five, to go back to school to study law and take bar exams.

A model student, Eduardo soon made himself popular with his professors and with fellow undergraduates, and his former career came in handy during university vacations, when Eduardo the Geek would become Freak once more, eating light bulbs, walking on glass and clamping his tongue in a mousetrap for a little extra cash to pay for his textbooks.

As much as he loved his new career, he admitted he found the law more bizarre than any freak show.

Famous failures

If you still need a little convincing that taking a risk or two in middle adulthood might be worth a try, take inspiration from some of the world's most famous one-time 'failures'.

Walt Disney's first cartoon company, Laugh-O-gram Films, made a spectacular loss and wound up in bankruptcy proceedings.

The Art of Failing Upwards

Michael Jordan, widely hailed as one of the greatest
basketball players of all time, was cut from his
varsity basketball team as a tenth grader
because he failed to stand out.

John Grisham, already a practising lawyer, tried
twenty-eight publishers before he persuaded one
small, barely known publishing house to take on his
first novel, *A Time To Kill*. His second novel, *The Firm*,
was a *New York Times* bestseller.

Early in her career, Marilyn Monroe failed to impress
20th Century Fox, who refused to renew her contract,
describing her as talentless
and unattractive.

The Tao of Dubya

If the world needs a better example of how the youthful fallen might still have a chance at becoming middle-aged and mighty, look no further than George W. Bush. As a young man, he had had a spectacular run of failed oil businesses under his belt, four in all, before turning to politics. Perhaps these early business failures inspired his razor-sharp observation that 'If we don't succeed, we run the risk of failure.' As US comedian Lewis Black commented, 'He's a man who was a failure until he was forty years old, which looks really good on your resumé – if you're a comic.'

'Your career begins with a bang, everyone thinks
you're wonderful, and then, with middle age,
something happens and you go into the wilderness.'

JEFFREY TATE

The Ageing Artist

*'Age only matters when one is ageing.
Now that I have arrived at a great
age, I might as well be twenty.'*

PABLO PICASSO

There are two related dilemmas associated with art and ageing. Firstly, if you are already an artist, actor or creative whatever, you may find that your powers are on the wane, or, at the very least, that those around you assume they must be. Secondly, if you always wanted to write, paint, sing or act, are your twilight years the optimal time to start? Are you ready to learn new tricks?

Either way, getting older is a great excuse for saying all the things you were too tactful or cowardly to say when you were younger ...

Seventy-five again!

One day in 1994, the actor and comedian Victor Borge announced, 'I'm celebrating my seventy-fifth birthday, which is sort of embarrassing, because I'm eighty-five.'

Time to get creative with the truth

Age can bring with it a new-found confidence to speak your mind and often this can be put to best effect when it's used creatively. Take, for example, Italian artist Maurizio Cattelan, known for his controversial works of art. Commissioned to produce a statue for the piazza in front of Milan's stock exchange, Cattelan didn't miss the opportunity to express exactly how he felt about the state of his country's finances. In fact, his finished work raised a finger to the financial quarter, quite literally: it was a 36-foot-high marble hand, the middle finger standing erect, positioned pointedly in front of the stock exchange. Journalists the world over couldn't fail to spot the message, leaving the artist himself with no need to express his viewpoint verbally.

That's one grumpy old git who found a new trick.

An awkward age

Some years ago, as a guest on *The Tonight Show with Jay Leno*, Arnold Schwarzenegger was asked by Leno whether he had had trouble training for his role in *Terminator 3*.

'I know what this is about – the age issue,' Schwarzenegger joked playfully. 'I'm fifty-five years old. It's an awkward age,' he acknowledged. 'You're thirty years too young to date Anna Nicole Smith, but you're thirty years too old to date Demi Moore!'

I'm still standing ... or am I?

Despite having reached seventy years of age, US actor Burt Reynolds was determined to do all his own stunts on the set of the 1998 thriller *Crazy Six*.

'Look, I can do this. I can still fall,' he told the film's producers. 'I just can't get up.'

Damned crickets

When the actor and director Mel Brooks was asked by an interviewer what he thought of critics, apparently he misheard the question, for he is said to have replied: 'They're very noisy at night. You can't sleep in the country because of them.'

It was only when the interviewer explained that he had asked about critics, not crickets, that Brooks corrected the mistake and said: 'Oh, critics! What good are they? They can't make music with their hind legs.'

Headless chicken

When you start forgetting your lines, like actor Paul Bailey apparently did when he appeared at Stratford-upon-Avon in *Richard III*, you know you're getting on in life.

In the production, Christopher Plummer was playing the title role while Bailey took the part of Lovell, who during Act III has to appear on stage and say the line, 'Here is the head of that ignoble traitor, the dangerous and unsuspected Hastings.'

However, on the night in question, Bailey completely forgot his line and instead simply stared at Plummer for what seemed like ages.

Eventually, Plummer had to help him out by asking, 'Is that the head of that ignoble traitor, the dangerous and unsuspected Hastings?'

To which Bailey simply replied, 'Yes.'

The likes of us

You know you're becoming an old dog when you're mistaken for a tramp, which is precisely what happened to author Sue Townsend, who wrote the Adrian Mole books and, at the time of this story, also had a play on in the West End of London.

One evening, she was outside a rather posh restaurant in St Martin's Lane in London looking through the window to see if her dinner guests had

arrived yet, when she was joined by a tramp carrying several plastic carrier bags and a large, open bottle of sherry, which he proceeded to slop all over the place.

As Sue continued to peer through the restaurant window, she heard the tramp whisper in her ear, 'Ah, it's not for the likes of us ...'

After you

Another way you know for sure you're entering your golden years is when everyone around you starts to look (and generally is) younger than you. Policemen seem to be about fifteen years old and doctors about twelve, so imagine the Hollywood director Billy Wilder's consternation when he was summoned to the studio by the 'movie brat' who had taken over as head.

'Great to meet you at last, Billy,' the youngster is supposed to have said. 'Hope you'll come on the team.

Believe we can make you some very interesting offers. Now, Billy, tell me – what have you done?'

Wilder is said to have paused a second and then replied politely: 'After you ...'

That old dog still had a bark.

Who is that man?

For many years, Groucho Marx and bestselling author Sidney Sheldon were close Hollywood friends and neighbours. In his eighties, Groucho was in the habit of popping round to visit Sheldon and his wife every afternoon for a snack of an apple and a chunk of cheese.

'It became such a ritual,' Sheldon recalled, 'that my wife and I looked forward to it every day.'

However, when the Sheldons decided to rent out their Hollywood mansion and move to Rome, confusion ensued.

One morning, Sidney received a letter from his tenant saying: 'We love the house, but there is one strange thing. Every afternoon, there is a little old man, between eighty-five and ninety, who knocks at our door and asks for some cheese and an apple. He's too well dressed for a tramp. Can you tell us who he is?'

Cutting-edge fashion

Elizabeth K, a Dutch fashion designer, was very excited
when she was given a once-in-a-lifetime opportunity to
take part in a prestigious New York fashion show at the
Guggenheim Museum. She worked for weeks on end
on her collection, perfecting her designs. Then, because
she didn't trust anyone else to make them, she did all
the sewing herself.

Day after day she sat in her studio, creating stunning
dresses and skirts, stitching feathers and sequins onto
the clothes by hand until, come the night of the show,
the models climbed into the garments. In order that
there was no VPL (visible panty line), Elizabeth K
insisted no underwear be worn. As the music began, the
models all started to parade down the catwalk, strutting
their funky stuff. Suddenly, the audience began wolf-
whistling and clapping. Elizabeth was pleased, but also
a little disconcerted.

Then she realized what she'd done. In her desperation
to get the collection finished on time, she'd forgotten
to sew any linings into the garments. With the catwalk
backlighting, everything was revealed. Needless to say,
the show was a great success – although it took the
models some time to appreciate exactly what it was that
everyone was applauding.

Worthy of notice

Finally, if you are pondering taking up art later in life, take heart from the words of the great artist Hokusai, in the postscript to his classic *One Hundred Views of Mt Fuji*, 1834:

'From the age of six I had a penchant for copying the form of things, and from about fifty, my pictures were frequently published; but until the age of seventy, nothing I drew was worthy of notice.

'At seventy-three years, I was somewhat able to fathom the growth of plants and trees, and the structure of birds, animals, insects and fish.

'Thus when I reach eighty years, I hope to have made increasing progress, and at ninety to see further into the underlying principles of things, so that at one hundred years I will have achieved a divine state in my art, and at one hundred and ten, every dot and every stroke will be as though alive.'

The Age of Anger

'I wouldn't say I was grumpy. It's more pathological – I have seismic tantrums. I get red in the face and cry at least three times a week, and I have to lie down and have a nap afterwards ... I'm in that late forties/ early fifties second toddlerhood phase.'

JENNY ECLAIR

Have you noticed how angry everyone is these days? It might be about lying politicians, inflation, the state of the world, global warming and wildfires, Trump, Brexit, transsexual rights, the neighbour's lawn, recycling bins, gun rampages ... Tick your favourites. It's as though the entire world is furious, and no one knows how to listen. However, at the same time, there is so much to be angry about. Idiotic TikTok fads, people who say 'should of' when they mean 'should have', people who are cruel to animals, the decline of *The Simpsons*, log-in verification codes, Hollywood's obsession with

superheroes ... and I'm just getting started.

Maybe we should just accept that the rest of the twenty-first century is going to be a period when everyone is furious and absolutely nothing is resolved as, for any real problem we face as a species, we will all line up in two teams shouting at each other. Anyone who suggests a reasonable compromise will be shunned and ignored like the Trojan princess Cassandra, the daughter of Priam who had the gift of prophecy but was fated always to be ignored.

Not feeling yourself?

Often, it's your attitude to life that reveals you as being old and grey, and there comes a time when moaning about the world around us suddenly becomes a daily occurrence.

This is obviously the case for ex-member of the rock group Yes, Rick Wakeman. At one time in his life, Wakeman was very cutting-edge, but now he reveals, 'My band call me Victor Meldrew. My kids call me Victor Meldrew. I actually think that when my hair finally falls out, I'll find that I probably am Victor Meldrew.'

Sweet dreams

In her early career, Germaine Greer was a radical thinker and feminist who placed the issue of gender firmly on the political agenda. At what moment was it that she began grumbling about Christmas cards, senior-style?

'The cards from people are fine,' she says, 'but the ones from organizations really piss me off. I get a card from the firm I once bought a sofa-bed from – "Merry Christmas, Germaine! From all at Slumbersoft." I don't want Merry Christmas from all at Slumbersoft, thank you very much.'

Tell me why I don't like coffee shops

Sir Bob Geldof, once such a rebellious fellow, now spends his time complaining about the decor in Starbucks, among other things. He has clearly fallen victim to the malaise that strikes us all in our later years: the need to moan about every single aspect of life itself. 'Starbucks makes pretty good coffee. That's got to be a good thing.

But it's all those newspapers and "Hey wow" coffee sofas, and the *pain au raisin* that goes with it that I can't stand,' rages Sir Bob. 'So the fact that you can get a decent cup of coffee in any high street – a good thing. All the bollocks that goes with it – f**k off.'

'Start every day off with a smile and get it over with.'

W.C. FIELDS

The underwear debate

If you want to know whether you're an old dog or not, ask yourself this: does the underwear you buy for yourself disappoint you to the extent that you would write to the manufacturer or to a newspaper to complain about it? If the answer is 'yes', then I'm afraid you're definitely on your way to senility. After all, aren't there more important things to be worrying about?

Not according to broadcaster and journalist Jeremy Paxman, who, in a private email (which was later leaked to the press) to Stuart Rose, then head of Marks & Spencer, laid bare some issues he had with M&S underwear:

'Like very large numbers of men in this country, I have always bought my socks and pants in Marks and Sparks. I've noticed that something very troubling

*has happened. There's no other way to put this. Their
pants no longer provide adequate support. When I've
discussed this with friends and acquaintances, it has
revealed widespread gusset anxiety.*

*'The other thing is socks. Even among those of us
who clip our toenails very rigorously, they appear to be
wearing out much more quickly on the big toe.*

*'Also, they are no longer ribbed around the top,
which means they do not stay up in the way they used
to. These are matters of great concern to the men in
Britain.'*

Nor, it seems, is Mr Paxman alone in his inability to
come to terms with modern underwear. Take, for
instance, the following rant by Lindsay Keir Wise, which
appeared in *The Oldie* magazine:

*'I am sure that I speak for others in what is a very
sensitive matter. The subject of my dissatisfaction
is men's underpants [...] When donning pants, one
must ascertain (a) which is the inside and which is the
outside and (b) which is the front and which is the back.
In doing this, one is guided by the label at the back of
the garment [...]*

*'In the cause of sartorial advancement, prompted
no doubt by the endorsement of a Beckham or Britney,
pants manufacturers have taken to applying the label,
hitherto the mark of orientation, not to the inside back*

but to the outside front! This intervention has disturbed the even tenor of my ways: I have not only found my underpants are inside out, but – if called to a public facility – that the exit hole is at the back ...'

These old dogs really haven't managed to get to the bottom of a new trick ...

Telling it like it is

Do you show no mercy when confronted with poor service? Do you impatiently correct ham-fisted answers on quiz shows? Are you goaded into noisy 'global warming' arguments? And, be honest, how many times have you written an angry post on Facebook about yet another piece of nonsense on TV?

This may sound suspiciously like the onset of grumpy old doggedness, but the chances are this is nothing new; maybe you're just as noisily resistant to convention as you've always been.

In fact, it's high time you celebrated your right to be stridently opinionated. So the next time anyone dares to tell you you're an old dog, don't be tempted to turn tactful! Stand up and tell it like it is.

Things it's now OK to hate:

- Anyone who begins their order at a coffee bar with the phrase, 'Can I get ...'
- People who use the term 'closure' in an attempt to sound emotionally in-tune
- Texting, tweeting and Face-ache
- Novelty ringtones
- Reality TV 'stars', talentless celebrities and anyone with a boob job or hair implants
- People who say 'share' when they mean 'tell'
- Office 'Secret Santas'
- Men who wear kilts to weddings, even though they're not really Scottish
- Discovering someone's put the cheese back into the fridge uncovered and now it's gone all crusty
- Doctors who make small talk during intimate examinations

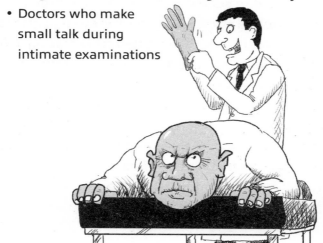

On the Bright Side

'Wisdom doesn't automatically come with old age. Nothing does – except wrinkles. It's true, some wines improve with age. But only if the grapes were good in the first place.'

ABIGAIL VAN BUREN

So, somehow, in spite of getting older and the world undoubtedly getting worse, we need to find ways to chill out. There may not be a whole lot of benefits to getting older, but, as the ultra-smooth French singer Maurice Chevalier once said, 'Old isn't so bad when you consider the alternative,' so maybe it's time to count your blessings.

One silver lining is a generous serving of extra wisdom. So perhaps it's time to stop grumbling about the 'youth of today' and instead embrace the wise old guru that lies deep within. It's time to learn a new trick and start giving others the benefit of your advice.

'Then there's a friend who only calls me when she's depressed. You all know people like this: I'm on the phone with her for three hours; it's a waste of time. She never listens to my advice – she will not jump.'

CAROL SISKIND

No time for loitering

One day in 1947, the author and journalist Wynford Vaughan-Thomas was invited to accompany the South African prime minister, Jan Smuts, on his 'morning stroll' up Table Mountain. Vaughan-Thomas reached the top of the mountain some ten minutes after Smuts, who was by then in his seventies.

'Young man,' Smuts said, 'at my age, I haven't as much time as you for loitering.'

What to do when you're all out of advice

When you yearn to be a shining beacon of wisdom, but you're all out of good advice, the best plan is to borrow someone else's ...

- 'Be nice to people on your way up because you'll meet them on your way down.' *Wilson Mizner*
- 'If you can't convince them, confuse them.' *Harry S. Truman*
- 'If it has tyres or testicles, you're going to have trouble with it.' *Linda Furney*
- 'Never believe in mirrors or newspapers.' *Tom Stoppard*
- 'Let me give you one word of advice: never go to a sex shop when you're horny. You have no idea what you're going to end up with – make a list; stick to the list.' *Wendy Spero*

The eternal optimist

The best advice is always that which has an intrinsic note of optimism. Woodie Held, an amiable baseball player through the 1950s, was famed among sporting circles for his upbeat, off-kilter advice. 'Don't forget to swing hard,' he would tell the players up to bat, 'in case you hit the ball.'

Dumb advice

Seeking professional advice doesn't always guarantee quality: things aren't always better just because you've paid more for them. Sometimes a bit of homespun wisdom goes a lot further. American comic Robert Kelly discovered this for himself after seeking therapy for problems in the bedroom: 'I go to therapy now, too. He's such an ass. He really is. I told him I had problems keeping it up during sex, and his advice was to look my girl right in the eyes while we're having sex. That's great. How am I going to think of other chicks when I'm staring right at her?'

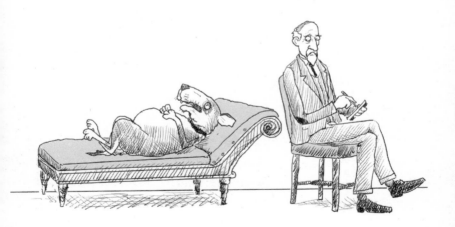

'A psychiatrist asks a lot of expensive questions your wife asks for nothing.'

JOEY ADAMS

Leave it to a professional?

In another example of professional advice backfiring in style, in 1999, rap artist Dr Dre consulted a musicologist to ascertain whether he could legally incorporate a five-note bass-line from a 1980s hit called 'Backstrokin' into his new track. Having been assured by the professional that he could go ahead, Dr Dre was nonetheless sued for infringement of copyright to the tune of $1.5 million.

So, in the end, the wisest suggestion may be P.G. Wodehouse's: 'I always advise people never to give advice.'

How Not
to Be a Bore

*'I can excuse everything but boredom. Boring
people don't have to stay that way.'*

HEDY LAMARR

It's a real fear of middle age, isn't it? That instead of imparting sage words of wisdom, we will begin to give voice to some of life's most excruciatingly dull thoughts. Dry rot and the price of kale have thus far been of little interest, but the terrifying thought that any day now, you might wake up with an involuntary need for this kind of conversational fodder can plague even the most vocally nimble of us.

How to tell if you're boring

An unoccupied mind can become a bored mind, and bored people are deadly dull, no matter what sex they

are. Often the problem is that the deadly dreary don't see how tedious they are to others. Ask yourself the following and find out whether you're one of life's great bores. If you're talking with friends, and decide to launch into one of your favourite stories or topics, how many of these statements apply?

- No one interrupts with 'Oh, that happened to me once!' or 'How funny, only the other day, I ...'
- At the start of your anecdote people are sitting or standing up straight, but by the end they have

relaxed into their chair, closer to horizontal than vertical, or else they stand slumped against walls and bar-tops

- Your companions pepper your story at odd intervals with short, empty phrases such as 'Oh really?' and 'How funny!'
- As you pause for breath, someone seizes the opportunity to steer you on to a whole new course, 'So, where did you go on holiday this year?'

If any or all of these statements apply to you, and if knowing that doesn't help you turn things around, perhaps the answer lies in technology. Scientists have now developed a tiny camera, small enough to be clipped surreptitiously onto your glasses and connected to a hand-held computer, which then uses face-recognition software to alert the speaker to signs of boredom or irritation in the listener. The Boredom Detector might sound a little extreme, but it could be the just the thing to save you from yourself.

Man bores woman

It's the big question: is becoming an old bore a painful inevitability? *Daily Mail* columnist Liz Hodgkinson felt that it absolutely is. Well, for men, at least. 'When did most men in my age group become so stupefyingly dull?' Liz wanted to know. 'I can foresee a time when there will be swathes of ditched older men living alone with only the crossword for company, while women of the same age are having the time of their lives. Gentlemen, you have been warned. It's time to smarten up your act or face a lonely old age.'

Not surprisingly, her warning didn't go unchallenged. Old codgers everywhere had something to say in their defence, but Michael Bywater of the *Independent* had the last word: 'We know things. We aren't obsessed with ourselves. We've realized we're no oil painting. We cook like gods. We know where to take you, and how to get in. We think *Grand Theft Auto* is for losers and abs are for narcissists and girls under twenty-two. We notice your ideas as well as your underwear, and enjoy your achievements as well as the way you smell of sugarcane and honey-of-rose ... Actually, we're better at most things except producing more testosterone than we can usefully channel.'

'Somebody's boring me. I think it's me.'
DYLAN THOMAS

Remembering Not to Forget

*'The advantage of a bad memory is
that one enjoys several times the same
good things for the first time.'*

FRIEDRICH NIETZSCHE

One of the great fears of ageing is the worry of losing our memory. Of course, dementia is a real possibility and not one that is funny in any way. But there is some humour to be found in the more mundane types of 'senior moments', in which we discover our memories are letting us down in petty ways, whether it is failing to recognize an acquaintance with a new haircut, not being able to remember where we put the car keys, or discovering our shirt has been buttoned up the wrong way all day.

Memorable telly

Most of us have childhood memories of finding one or other of our parents at the top of the stairs, a bewildered look on their face, muttering to themselves, 'Now, what did I come up here for?' Sadly, we will fall victim to precisely these moments ourselves, sooner or later. American comedian John Heffron is already there. 'They always say that the older you get, you start to lose your memory,' he says. 'I could be watching a TV show for forty-five minutes. Then, during commercials, I start flipping through the channels. Then I have to stop and go, "What the hell was I watching?"'

Splashing around

According to his wife, novelist G.K. Chesterton was renowned for having odd lapses of memory – none more so than on one particular day when he had gone to take a bath. Standing outside the bathroom door, she heard him get out of the tub, after which there was a long interval and then a loud splashing noise.

Apparently, Chesterton had forgotten that he'd already bathed and had sat back in the bath again. On realizing his error, his wife then heard him exclaim: 'Damn, I've been here before!'

Over the rainbow

The late TV broadcaster Hugh Scully must have known all about feeling his age, for at the end of a BBC television interview with Liza Minnelli on the programme *Nationwide*, he ended the Q-and-A session by saying, 'Thank you, Judy Garland.'

Luckily, Minnelli was on good form that day and saved the moment by replying, 'I'll tell Liza.'

Déjà vu?

Renowned for his absent-mindedness, the former publisher of the *New York Post*, J. David Stern, was once hurrying down the street when he bumped into an old friend, who invited him for lunch. Stern agreed, although he asked if they could go to a nearby restaurant as he was already running late.

They entered the establishment and sat down at a table, but when it came to making an order, Stern couldn't understand why he didn't feel very hungry.

'I beg your pardon, sir,' said the waiter, 'but you just finished lunch five minutes ago.'

Losing your bearings

Another aspect of forgetfulness is the very real possibility of getting lost.

Some people know they're past their prime when they forget where they've put their car keys, others when they forget where they've parked the car, but one woman caused mayhem when she drove for fifteen miles up the wrong side of the M65 motorway.

According to an article in *The Times*, the woman became confused when confronted with a 'new traffic configuration' at a roundabout. Police followed the car for seven junctions until they could bring her to a halt around Barrowford in Lancashire.

In mitigation, she explained, 'There was nowhere to turn around.'

The greatest own goal ever?

In October 1964, one of the greatest sporting gaffes of all time was perpetrated by American football star Jim Marshall of the Minnesota Vikings. The Vikings were playing against the San Francisco 49ers, when Marshall suddenly took hold of the ball and began running the wrong way up the pitch. Oblivious to the fact that none of his opponents seemed in any way anxious to stop him and ignoring his own teammates, who were hollering at him to stop or at the very least turn around, Marshall eventually reached the goal line, where he scored two points ... for the 49ers.

To eat or not to eat

The Nobel Prize-winning chemist Harold Urey (1893–1981), who was famed for his forgetfulness, was stopped in the street by a friend of his one sunny afternoon. After a brief conversation, the men began to go their separate ways – until, that is, Urey turned round and asked: 'John, which way was I walking when I met you?'

His friend pointed him in the right direction.

'Oh good,' said Urey, 'that means I've already had my lunch!'

Ladies and gentlemen

Not knowing where you are is usually the preserve of explorers who have lost their compass and maps, but occasionally, it is an early indication that you are past it, as the following anecdote suggests.

A woman entered a room in a London hotel, where she immediately recognized a well-known British politician pacing up and down, up and down. The woman asked the gentleman what he was doing there.

'I'm about to give an after-dinner speech,' he said.

'And do you always get so nervous before you're called upon to deliver them?' she asked, not unreasonably.

'Nervous?' he replied. 'I'm not nervous. In fact, I never get nervous.'

'Then what are you doing,' demanded the woman, 'in the ladies' room?'

Some wise thoughts

American politicians have never been known for their intellect; in fact, quite a few of them have been in office while dangerously 'senior'. Indeed, in the current political climate, the two main parties seem intent on supplying candidates for the presidency who have already outlived Methuselah.

One such politician, Senator Bob Dole, was notorious for his lapses of memory, particularly when giving speeches. One day, for example, he was trying to explain to an interviewer the problems politicians faced keeping their private lives private.

'You read what Disraeli had to say,' Dole said, and then paused for quite a time. 'I don't remember what he said. He said something.' Another long pause, then: 'He's no longer with us.'

Lost for words

You know you're an old dog when your mind goes completely blank – but never is this more inopportune than when people are waiting to hear what you have to say, as happened to another American politician, John G. Winant.

Once, when asked to make a speech in England, Winant stood in agonized silence for four minutes, before finally whispering: 'The worst mistake I ever made was in getting up in the first place.'

That's definitely an old dog moment.

Love and Marriage

'I think a lot about getting old. I don't want to be one of those seventy-year-olds who still wants lots of sex.'

RUPERT EVERETT

The notion that beyond your twenties you're at daily risk of becoming sexually 'past it' is drummed into us by an advertising industry obsessed with youth. Evidently, by this time of life, we should all be far more interested in golf and gardening than getting down and dirty in the sack. But while Boy George may not be alone in preferring a nice cup of tea to a raunchy all-nighter in the bedroom, clearly he's in a minority.

It's well known that women don't reach their sexual peak until their thirties (perhaps much later) and older couples, liberated by their empty nests, can celebrate their love as noisily as they like. So if you fancy embracing promiscuity with all the vigour of middle youth, cast aside your sudoku and drop your allotment overalls.

Haven't you heard? There is sex after twenty-five! But some old dogs haven't learned new tricks ...

Straight-talking

In modern times, it seems that almost anything goes. You've got your eye on a man or woman half your age? Fine. You want an open relationship? Knock yourself out. All that matters is that you speak your mind. So when a successful divorcee in his late sixties asked his beautiful thirty-something girlfriend to marry him, he was delighted that she accepted. Still cautious, however, he insisted on a prenuptial agreement but agreed happily to most of her requests.

Her house would remain her house, she insisted. 'Naturally,' he said. The convertible he bought her last birthday – she wouldn't have to give it up should the marriage come to an end? 'Absolutely not,' he assured her. As for their sex life, her interests would need protecting in this department too. She wanted to be sure her needs would be met – at least six times a week. 'No problem,' he replied, affably. 'Book me in for Saturdays.'

Whatever turns you on …

Every once in a while, a story of sexual endeavour hits the news. Take, for instance, forty-something mother of three, Julie Amiri. She was arrested for shoplifting on London's Oxford Street. And it wasn't her first time. In fact, she had a track record of a staggering fifty-two similar offences. What stirred Julie to steal wasn't poverty, greed or malice. For Julie, the experience of being detained by security guards and arrested by uniformed police was entirely, irresistibly intoxicating. In fact, she convinced doctors that it was the only way she could achieve orgasm, and as a result she escaped without a single conviction.

Love and Marriage

> 'When you've been married for a while it gets a bit
> boring in bed. The other day I said to my husband,
> "I can't remember the last time we had sex."
> 'He yelled back, "We're having it now!"'

VICTORIA WOOD

Every heartbeat

Towards the end of her life, the actress Sarah Bernhardt lived in a top-floor apartment in Paris. One day, a fan of hers paid her a call, but became very out of breath having climbed up innumerable steps to get there.

'Madame,' he said, 'why do you live so high up?'

'My dear friend,' Bernhardt replied, 'it is the only way I can still make the hearts of men beat faster.'

> 'One of the consequences of growing older, I find,
> is that you become progressively less interested in
> other people's sex lives. These days, frankly, I find
> it difficult to show much interest even in my own.'

MARTIN KELLNER

The joy of marriage

Getting irritated with your spouse is par for the course, but you really know you're getting on in life when you start telling others just how irritating your partner can be.

Such was the case when the actress Shirley MacLaine asked Samuel Goldwyn's wife, Frances, what it was like being married to the same man for more than thirty-five years.

'It gets worse every day,' replied Mrs Goldwyn. 'Thirty-five years ago, I told Sam to come home and I'd fix him lunch. He's been coming home for lunch every day for thirty-five years!'

Empty nest

US comedian Jeff Allen knows that the demands of a busy family life can mean that years go by without the two of you having a chance to get away together. So Jeff was delighted when, for the first time in more than ten years, he and his wife booked a child-free trip to Hawaii.

'So you parents know, after ten years, by the second day in Hawaii, we had no idea how to entertain ourselves. By the third day, we went to the beach and did what came naturally to us. We started yelling at other people's kids.'

Till death us do part?

Divorce can be a costly business and some guys will go to any lengths to get out of paying alimony. In 2008 a Connecticut couple stood in the divorce courts after twenty-six years of marriage.

Karen Finnegan cited irreconcilable differences in her suit against her husband, Joseph. But Joe wasn't prepared to pay up without a fight. He claimed that she couldn't file for divorce because a heart failure – a temporary death – some years previously was enough to dissolve his marriage. He filed a motion captioned 'Motion to Dismiss on the Grounds that the Defendant is No Longer Married to the Plaintiff Having Been Previously Completely, Although Not Permanently Dead'.

The motion was denied, on the basis that Joe's 'death' did not match up to the necessary legal definition of 'permanent' and 'irreversible cessation' of life. Nice try, Joe.

'Marriage is forever. It's like cement.'

PETER O'TOOLE

Valentine's Day

Comedian Michael McIntyre was once discussing the topic of Valentine's Day and the associated rituals, saying, 'You have to come up with this shit every year. Last week I just wrote, "I still love you, see last year's card for full details."'

Truly worthy of an old dog who hasn't learned new tricks.

A not-so-spiritual break-up

Custody battles can be the most devastating part of divorce, but not all battles are fought over the children. When Hollywood couple Meg Ryan and Dennis Quaid separated, citing irreconcilable differences, their struggle for custody was not fought over their son Jack, then only eight years old, but over something far more bizarre. The *LA Times* reported that the couple were filing for exclusive access rights to their guru and spiritual leader, Gurumayi Chidvilasananda. Both were reported as having been described by a close friend as 'guru-dependent', but the court refused to rule on access to professional services and Ryan and Quaid were left to seek enlightenment elsewhere.

At least a mid-life crisis about mysticism is probably better than one about money!

In the doghouse

Every marriage has its ups and downs, and at some point in the relationship one of you is bound to end up sleeping on the couch. But forty-eight-year-old Vlad Popescu from Romania pushed his wife Maria to the edge of endurance with his heavy drinking and indolent ways. He was so slovenly, Maria complained to the press, that the closest he'd got to doing any work in ten years was to build a dog kennel. So she booted him out of the house and into the dog kennel. Vlad complained of sub-zero temperatures but Maria was reportedly unmoved, saying, 'His boozing has made our family's life a misery until now and it's about time he woke up and experienced some of the consequences.'

'A good marriage would be between a blind wife and a deaf husband.'

MICHEL DE MONTAIGNE

Battle of the sexes

If there's one thing you should have learned by now, it's that the battle of the sexes never really ends. Whether it's fought on a tennis court or over who comes out on top in the boardroom or the bedroom, the parameters of the battleground may change with passing years, but the fight goes on. The only way through it is to look for the funny side.

What he says:

'Men are far more romantic about women. Men are the ones who'll say, "I've found somebody. She's amazing. If I don't get to be with this person, I can't carry on. If I'm not with her I'll end up in a bedsit, I'll be an alcoholic." That's how women feel about shoes.'

DYLAN MORAN

'I've got no problem buying tampons. I'm a modern man. But apparently, they're not a "proper present".'

JIMMY CARR

Love and Marriage

'I thought when I was forty-one I would be married with kids. Well, to be honest, I thought I'd be divorced with weekend access.'

SEAN HUGHES

What she says:

'Why did God create men? Because vibrators can't mow the lawn.'

MADONNA

'I don't want to be married just to be married. I can't think of anything lonelier than spending the rest of my life with someone I can't talk to, or worse, someone I can't be silent with.'

MARY ANN SHAFFER

'Women speak because they wish to speak, whereas a man speaks only when driven to speech by something outside himself – like, for instance, he can't find any clean socks.'

JEAN KERR

'To attract men, I wear a perfume called New Car Interior.'

RITA RUDNER

Splitting your assets

It's always nice to read about that rare breed of lawsuit, the amicable divorce, where the couple readily agree terms and split their assets fifty-fifty, fair and square. When forty-two-year-old Moeun Sarim from rural Cambodia suspected his wife of having an affair with a local police officer, he demanded a divorce. The settlement included the agreement that Sarim would take half the marital home – literally. In the presence of legal witnesses, Sarim and various family members arrived with saws and proceeded to remove precisely half the house, taking the debris away to his parents' home nearby. His wife, who denied having had an affair at all, nonetheless gave in to her ex-husband's demands, describing the settlement as 'very strange'. Anything for a quiet life.

Tough love

Is divorce too easy these days? Those who've been through it would probably disagree, but there are plenty out there who will argue that couples need to try harder to make their marriages work instead of running straight to the lawyer's office at the first sign of trouble. US comedian Wanda Sykes has come under exactly this pressure, explaining how her mother reacted to the news that she was getting divorced. 'Let me tell you something – your father and I had a shoot-out, OK? He took one in the arm – Harry, show her where I shot you – now, see, that's love right there. You gotta learn how to work these things out. He was wrong, I shot him – you move on.'

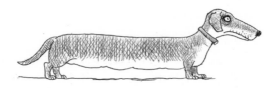

Back to the Metaverse

'The greatest thing about Facebook,
is that you can quote something and
totally make up the source.'

GEORGE WASHINGTON

Yet another sign of impending old age is when technology starts to leave you behind, something that *Private Eye* editor Ian Hislop seems to know all about.

'People tell me that blogs are the future. Oh well, maybe I won't be part of it. I've re-designed the website of *Private Eye* so that when you go on, there's a big message that flashes up, which says: "Go and buy the magazine."'

Sounds like one old dog who definitely won't be learning a new trick. Ah, technology! There's nothing that comes close to it for its ability to infuriate.

Spam email

The unwanted mail that used to pour through your letter box was simple to understand: gas bills, party invitations, and – if you bought something from a catalogue – yet another catalogue offering products of interest solely to retired people with the time to ponder buying a collapsible snow shovel for the car. All this junk meant that you had to shoulder barge the door open when you got home from holiday. Still, you got to use the recycling bags the council dropped off.

Declutter

Email, far from replacing all this clutter, has actually increased the chaos. The gas company now feels obliged to email you a note that your bill is coming, a reminder that your payment is overdue and – somewhat optimistically – a customer satisfaction survey, along with a personal note from the managing director explaining their commitment to customer service (and higher prices). In place of the party invitation, your friends expect you to commit to parties on Facebook or, even worse, to endure a fourteen-minute, poorly animated digital card on your birthday.

Tick the box

Some spam is bearable. We can live with the odd offer of

a foolproof way to lengthen our manhood or a wonder drug promising unlimited sexual prowess. But forget to tick the box to unsubscribe from email updates when you buy something online and you'll be receiving emails packed with last-minute offers from the florists for the rest of time.

And guess what? It's not getting any easier to read things on the screen so you'll be printing them out as well.

Feeling like an old dog yet?

Google Maps with Street View

At the touch of button you can use Google Maps to see streets and houses all over the world, the north and south poles and even the surface of the moon. For someone as poor at directions as you, the whole thing has been a boon. No longer are you late for meetings, as you wander aimlessly up and down some strange road looking for a client's ambiguously named office block. You've also discovered that it is great for scoping out if the hotel you've booked online is actually wedged between a brothel and dogs' home before you get there. However, not everyone shares your enthusiasm.

A man in the village of Angers, France, is suing Google for ten thousand euros, arguing that the image the technology giant put online of him urinating in his back yard violated his right to privacy and ruined his reputation in the community. But taking a whiz in your backyard is tame by Street View standards. Google has also captured hundreds of bizarre images such as an apparently naked man emerging from the boot of a car, couples snogging, crimes in progress and a host of men furtively entering 'adult entertainment' stores.

Password protection

It's hard to know which faceless technocrat decided it was a good idea to password-protect everything that you might reasonably want to access in the course of your day. But nowadays your laptop, mobile phone, office network, gas bill and your spouse are held behind military-grade, 256-bit encryption. While it is reassuring that hackers can't access your overdraft, it is absolutely infuriating that you can't either.

Random characters

Most of us struggle to recall our own postcode so it seems crazy that we're expected to deal with baffling combinations of letters, numbers and random characters issued by everyone from our car insurers to the supermarket. As a result we've all stopped caring. According to Mark Burnett's book *Perfect Passwords: Selection, Protection, Authentication*, the world's most used password is '123456'. Number two on the list is simply 'password'.

All a blur

While Google routinely blurs the faces of people captured by their Street View cameras, it can be argued that clothing, local knowledge and the fact that they are relieving themselves in the garden of a house they own makes them pretty recognizable.

Google Street View is a bit like the local newspaper. You secretly harbour a desire to appear in it and wave coyly as a Google car goes by. You just wish they had given you adequate notice, for when you check your home on Street View, you are embarrassed by what you see. The bins are overflowing, the front garden is alive with weeds, the windows hang open like a teenager's mouth and the whole place needs a paint job. Thanks to pin-sharp digital photography, the house you pay a fortune to the mortgage company for looks like it's one up from a squat. No wonder your friends never come to visit.

Remember you're a Womble

The solution is surely to give us just one password that works for everything. In fact, your parents should select this for you at birth and insist it be tattooed – backwards so it can be read in a mirror – on your forehead. And if walking around with 'womblefiend123' on your face in Gothic script seems a high price to pay, remember that at least you'll be able to check your bank balance.

Of course, so will every thief and scammer in the world!

Social media

Research has shown that the huge growth in use of social media has been fuelled not by tech-obsessed youngsters but by two groups who really should know better: thirty-five to forty-five-year olds and those over sixty. The basic offering of social media is keeping in touch and sharing your experiences. This makes some sense when applied to those under thirty-five who are getting out to bars and clubs, dating new people and going on exciting backpacking holidays, but how does it work for you? You spend the majority of your time at work and the rest slumped in front of the telly. You never go out and when you do it's only to attend a dinner party with people you've spent so much time with you could draw a map detailing every line on their ageing faces.

This lack of activity hasn't stopped you getting heavily involved in social media. You dutifully signed up for accounts with Twitter, Facebook, TikTok and Instagram; installed the apps on your phone and spent a heady evening making connections with friends, friends of friends, family members and, in some cases, people's children and pets.

You are tremendously excited by the sense of purpose setting up these accounts has given to your humdrum existence, but you find that you hit a block when it comes to actually sharing information because a life in which the highlight of the week is ordering a Chinese takeaway from the Golden Panda on a Friday night is hardly worth reporting.

Strictly old school

Luckily, your new best friends seem happy to supply the solution to this problem. Despite the fact that they're always in when you call and are usually watching the same TV shows as you are, on social media they have managed to post the evidence of a glittering existence of weddings, gigs, old school reunions and laughter-filled family outings. It isn't long before you stop trying to post the embarrassing truth about your own life and devote yourself to living vicariously through their online adventures.

On social media, everything looks more vital and

exciting than it actually is. Even the events that you attended in person, when reflected through the prism of other people's opinion, are wildly improved. A night which you remember as being defined by someone spilling red wine down your front, awful food and your best friend confiding in you that they were thinking of getting divorced, looks like a kaleidoscopic joyfest on Facebook. Furious minute-by-minute reporting of key points at conferences by tweeting colleagues seem like a much better version of events than you sitting at the back of the conference hall wondering when the next coffee break is.

One informal survey posted by research group Forrester revealed that 56 per cent of people felt that the time they spent on social media was wasted. You would beg to differ. Unless things start getting more interesting in your life soon, social media may become all that stands between you and suicide.

Call of Duty

Once a trip to your local record shop promised a relaxing afternoon nostalgically browsing through discounted CDs of classic albums; eventually, it offered nothing but a minor panic attack when you found yourself lost between row upon row of garishly packaged video games. Now you don't even have that joy as the record store closed down years ago and was replaced by a nail bar.

It's hard to think of anything more disruptive to one's sanity and sleeping patterns than video games. While playing them is bad, it pales into insignificance against the horror of living with someone who does.

Of these digitized tributes to mindlessly obsessive behaviour, none is more irritating to the sane person than *Call of Duty*. For almost twenty years, *Call of Duty* and its many unimaginatively titled sequels (*Call of Duty* 2, *Call of Duty* 3 etc.) have gripped every male under the age of forty with the kind of fervour previously reserved for Premier League football.

Call of Duty is a first-person shooter, which means that the player experiences the action via a set of disembodied hands holding a gun which pumps an endless stream of bullets into screaming soldiers or screaming zombies. For anyone living with the player, this virtual bloodbath will be experienced solely through a nerve-shattering cacophony of groans, explosions and muted gunfire coming from the next room.

As of 2022, the makers of this tribute to testosterone-fuelled madness announced that the franchise had already sold 400 million copies. Something must be done. That means that there are at least 400 million deeply unhappy spouses, parents and female siblings sitting on the sofa with their hands over their ears trying to get on the telly to watch *The X Factor*.

The ringtone draw

There are three kinds of mobile phone owners: people like you who get a new phone and leave it exactly as it is; people who get a new phone and fiddle with the settings to change the ringtone; and then there are the downloaders of ringtones. This last group also create their own wallpapers, customize its vibrations and put the thing in a novelty case that makes it look more like a child's craft project than a communication device.

Most parents use pictures of their children as a screen saver on their phone but when the kids turn thirteen this has to stop: a forty-five-year-old man with a photograph of a smiling fifteen-year-old in a bathing costume on his phone will find himself in a police cell long before he can explain that it's an innocent picture of his daughter on a family holiday.

While you have nothing against those who wish to personalize their phones, you accepted a long time ago that you are too lazy and too inept to change the ringtone on your phone. You got your first mobile back when they were relatively rare and primarily owned by drug dealers, rent boys and the middle management with abusive bosses who were prepared to pay outrageous call charges to harangue their staff in the middle of the night. In those glorious days it was novelty ringtones that made the veins on your neck bulge, but as mobiles have become ubiquitous it is the out-of-the-box ringtone that has become the scourge of your day.

Is it for me?

Despite the phone companies offering us ever-increasing ways to personalize our phones, most of us have no inclination to do so. As a result, everyone has the same ringtone. So when a phone rings on any train or in a meeting, the chances are it could be an incoming call for any one of four people sitting within a five-yard radius of one another. This is fantastic when the call is for you but unbelievably humiliating when you're the one who eagerly grabs their phone to discover it's not.

Despite the fact that everyone perks up like a gang of meerkats when a phone starts ringing, no one will risk reaching for their phone for fear of embarrassment. You find yourself in a Mexican stand-off, unsure whether you should be the first to go for your phone and risk looking like a fool. It goes without saying that by the time someone finally cracks, the caller has rung off.

'Technological progress has merely provided us with more efficient means for going backwards.'

ALDOUS HUXLEY

Music on mobiles

It is the duty of the young to annoy the old. While the dress sense of today's teens is annoying – trousers worn beneath the buttocks (boys) or horrible velvet tracksuits (girls) – it pales into insignificance compared to their love of listening to music on their mobile phones.

If you happen to travel on a bus or train during daylight hours, the chances are there will be at least one group of under-eighteens listening to drill music through the woefully inadequate single speaker of a mobile phone. The music itself is terrible and seems to consist of an incessant hissing more reminiscent of a malfunctioning kettle, interspersed with repetitive bleeps and random shouting. The lyrics, such as they are, often extol the virtues of driving a Mercedes for an audience whose only source of income is pocket money.

The horribly tinny sound is not a concern to young people. But thanks to a condition known as presbycusis, the ability to hear high frequencies deteriorates in people over the age of twenty-five. This condition was used to devastating effect in 2008 with the launch of the Mosquito Alarm. This was an electronic device that could be used to deter loitering young people by emitting a sound of approximately 17.4 kHz – a frequency that is ear-piercing to them but undetectable to their elders and betters.

New smartphone

The phone companies like to issue a newer, shinier and sexier handset a couple of weeks after you got your last one so yours ends up looking like an obsolete brick that even Thomas Edison would have been ashamed to be seen with. It's a long, painful, contractually designated twenty-four-month wait until you can upgrade to something state of the art. By the time you get round to the latest folding screen technology, the tech will have moved on again, possibly to a screen you can roll up so it looks like a Swiss roll.

Despite the fact that your old phone works perfectly

well, you're pretty confident that investing in a wafer-thin, glass and metal slab which looks like a prop from *Star Trek* will impress work colleagues and the opposite sex alike with just how digitally savvy you are.

However, as soon as you pop the cellophane on its gleaming white box and your ludicrously exciting new gizmo drops effortlessly into your palm, it dawns on you that everything else you own is designed to destroy it. House keys will score great canyons into its screen, half-eaten boiled sweets will clog up its nano grills, pocket fluff will bespoil its sheen. While it won't fit comfortably into the pocket of your jeans, it will fit neatly into the mouth of a child or small dog. Even your sweaty fingers leave unsightly greasy marks on the graphite.

So it's back to the mobile phone shop you go to spend another fifty pounds on cases, covers and screen guards which make your lovely new phone look like something you picked up cheap at a Tupperware party.

You're getting too old for new tricks when ...

- Your short-term memory has been replaced by a notepad and pen ... but you can't remember where you put them
- Conversations with people your own age often turn into 'duelling ailments'
- You go to the dictionary to look up a word, spend minutes locating it, then realize you're staring down at the word 'dictionary'
- Your friends compliment you on your new alligator shoes ... but you're barefoot
- Your best friend is dating someone half their age – and isn't breaking any laws
- You feel like the morning after, but did nothing the night before
- You can live without sex, but not without your glasses
- You have all the time in the world to put your snapshots in photo albums, but you have no idea who the people in the photos are

- Your childhood toys are now in a museum
- You're on the floor cleaning or playing with the kids when the phone rings, and it's just easier to crawl to the phone than to get up and walk there

'It is only when they go wrong that machines remind you how powerful they are.'

CLIVE JAMES

The Old Age Traveller

'Don't just rule out going on a cruise.
Think about it, then rule it out.'

JENNY ECLAIR

For those with more free time and some spare cash, it's probably time to think about taking a holiday. But don't let anyone lure you onto a cruise ship just yet. There's still plenty of time to dream bigger than just an all-you-can-eat supper at the captain's table. Of course, in the age of social media influencers posting their TikToks from the top of K2, on safari in the Serengeti, or from the South Pole, you can forget trying to impress anyone with your holiday snaps. But there is still plenty to be gained from the joys of travel, including but not limited to snake bites, interesting new viral illnesses, and an empty bank account.

There are also plenty of new tricks that have to be

learned, or at least navigated around, if we want to keep the grumpiness level down.

The quiet carriage

Have you travelled on a train lately? Assuming you can work out a ticketing system that is so complex it feels like the train company hired cryptographers to design it, you still have to face cancellations, delays and navigating a station forecourt that looks like a refugee camp.

When you finally get on the train, you find it so clogged with discarded fast-food wrappers and bottles that the carriages look more like the aftermath of a teenage sleepover than a modern transportation system. The seats are small and the less said about the toilets the better.

The most irritating thing about modern train travel is the constant and mindless use of mobile devices by the passengers. The most taxing hazard you used to face on the train was accidentally sitting down opposite a table full of squaddies making their way through a mountain of canned lager. Now, as soon as the train pulls out of the station, everyone takes out their mobile and rabbits on about being on the train and what time they're arriving, as if this information is of national importance.

To seek some relief, you try to position yourself in the quiet carriage. Supposedly an oasis of peace, this is right at the far end of the train which means you have to sprint the length of the platform to make it. Far from being an oasis of peace, the quiet carriage is deafeningly loud. The proud owners of mobile technology now find themselves at a loose end and talk loudly about how they really must make a call, as soon as they arrive, to their fellow travellers, the conductor and – if all else fails – themselves.

Low-cost airlines

Like a rain-sodden barbecue or mosquito bite on your eyelid, a miserable trip on a low-cost airline has become a regular feature of your summer. The boom in low-cost air travel created a corresponding boom in the number of numpties, children and pensioners clogging up our airports. Air travel has changed from a glamorous cosmopolitan escape to the transport equivalent of a long weekend at a holiday camp.

You love to go abroad but you also love a bargain. So, as you book your summer holidays you put aside all the terrible experiences you have previously had with low-cost airlines, resolutely ignore your partner's pleadings and allow yourself to be seduced once again by the offer of flights for spare change.

The first thing you discover is that unless you are planning to travel in two years' time, the flight actually costs much more. And then you start to add the extras ... If you want to bring a bag (or your kids), book a seat, arrive at your destination earlier than midnight or pay with a credit card, you have to pay more. As boarding a low-cost airline is a high-speed scramble reminiscent of the Pamplona bull run, you might like to pay for early boarding (effectively a head start), too.

'Countries are actually closer than you think ...
Pilots just fly aeroplanes around longer
to make you think they're far away.'

BILL BAILEY

Early riser

As a matter of policy, all planes operated by low-cost airlines run late so you will spend at least an hour waiting in a hideously decorated Day-Glo holding area before boarding. As you had to get up at 5.30 a.m. to check-in, you'll be pretty hungry by the time you get on the plane. Naturally there's no complimentary food on board, so you can look forward to paying Michelin-starred prices for food which resembles something lurking around the back of the bins at KFC. The indifferent, demoralized staff deliver it to your seat then attempt to sell you a lottery ticket.

You will arrive at your economy villa hot, hungry, three hundred quid lighter and clutching a piece of paper which promises to return your bags from wherever in the world they have ultimately been delivered. At this point you promise yourself never to take a low-cost airline again ... until next year, that is.

*'Airplane travel is nature's way of making
you look like your passport photo.'*

AL GORE

Automated check-in

When it comes to travelling the friendly skies, people are fast going out of fashion in the customer service department. It's possible to book and pay for a flight online without talking to anyone, then you drive yourself to the airport and check yourself and your bags in using an automated terminal, before following further instructions on a screen to get you through the departure lounge and onto the plane.

When you finally park at a short stay car park that costs more than your actual ticket and is situated three miles from the terminal, you are already cutting it fine. As a result you pass a tense fifteen minutes looking at your watch as you wait for the shuttle bus to the terminal.

Still worrying about whether you're going to be landing at midnight the same day or lunchtime the following day, you arrive at the terminal to be greeted by a confused mob wandering aimlessly around the departure hall like something from a George A. Romero movie.

Some are staring blankly at the machines wondering whether they should be using their boarding pass or their passport to check-in, while others are stabbing wildly at the touchscreen and arguing with their partner over which seat number is the bulkhead and whether they will have to pay more for it. A separate, more desperate group has detached itself and is trying to deposit their bags. This means alternating between the information desk and magazine store because they are the only places where they can see a human being in uniform.

You make it into the departure lounge and queue up for a coffee. It is then that you notice on the monitor that your flight has already been called, even though it is not leaving imminently. The reason for this is made clear by a small sign next to the monitor warning you that your designated gate is a twenty-five minute walk away. Unless you run, spilling boiling hot coffee down your front as you go, the plane will be gone by the time you arrive.

It's pretty clear that all this hassle could be averted if there was a nice young person in a beret and blazer to tell you where to go, but airlines have removed them

all in favour of a sequence of processes, automated notifications and oblique signs worthy of *The Da Vinci Code*. Ironically, the one place they have kept a uniformed person – the cockpit – is the one place they don't need one. Modern airliners have had the ability to fly on autopilot from one airport to another without the need for human intervention since the 1970s. Shame they can't say the same about the passengers.

> *'What does it mean to pre-board?*
> *Do you get on before you get on?'*
>
> **GEORGE CARLIN**

Travelling light

If you think the worst part of travelling is packing your luggage, perhaps you could join the growing numbers of people who are tempted to take a 'nakation' at a nudist resort. So long as you remember to slap the sunblock on the parts where the sun doesn't normally shine, all should be well.

At least, that was US comedian Carol Leifer's hope. She confessed: 'Thought it would be all sexy and hot. Oh my God, what a flubber-fest! Everybody who shouldn't be naked is naked – didn't make me want to take off my clothes, made me want to take out my contacts.'

*'Good morning all. I am still in Florida where it
is hot and lovely. And sticky, which isn't so great
at my age. Too many creases to wipe dry.'*

TWEET FROM JONATHAN ROSS

Big mistake

Forgetting your passport when you're going on holiday
is not a good idea, nor is leaving your bag on a bus, but
one violinist took forgetfulness to real extremes when
he had an old dog moment and left £180,000 worth of
seventeenth-century Italian violin on a train luggage
rack.

'I thought I couldn't possibly forget it,' he said. 'It
was just one of those terrible moments when I realized,
as the train was steaming off, that I had.'

If in doubt ...

If you are still contemplating travelling round the world,
or fulfilling your bucket list of places to visit before you
die, here's some advice from a few of those who have
gone before you:

*'If God had intended us to fly, he wouldn't
have invented Spanish air traffic control.'*

CRAIG CHARLES

'There are two kinds of travel: first
class and with children.'

JULIAN BARNES

'If forced to travel on an aeroplane, try to get
in the cabin with the captain, so you can keep
an eye on him and nudge him if he falls
asleep or point out any mountains looming up ahead.'

MIKE HARDING

'There is nothing more grotesque
to me than a vacation.'

DUSTIN HOFFMAN

'I wouldn't mind seeing China if I
could come back the same day.'

PHILIP LARKIN

Ill-fated adventurers

You've packed the kids off so that it's just the two of you.
You checked out the hotel reviews, did your research,
chose the best time of year to travel; in fact, you've done
everything right. And yet circumstances way beyond

your control not only conspire to wreck your vacation but send governments into crisis management.

Take, for example, the middle-aged Swiss couple drawn to the stunning azure skies and turquoise ocean of the Maldives; the perfect site to renew their wedding vows after a long and happy marriage. But the ceremony resulted in a political furore after a video of the ceremony was posted on YouTube. The celebrant, addressing the couple in the local language, chanted what sounded like a prayer and a blessing; in fact, his homage to the happy couple transpired to be a torrent of abuse, accusing them of fornication and bestiality, packed with lewd sexual references and heaping insults on the couple's children.

The video went viral, the celebrant was duly arrested and the Maldives government went into diplomatic overdrive. But the lesson for all romantics out there looking to renew their vows in exotic locations – make sure you know exactly what you're saying 'I do' to!

A tip from Tommy Cooper

If you ever find yourself on a flight you can't afford, in the middle of the worst turbulence ever, on your way to a destination you know you won't enjoy, you could always try to liven things up ... Here's the great comedian's thoughts: 'It's strange, isn't it? You stand in the middle of a library and go, "Aaaaagghhhh," and everyone just stares at you. But you do the same thing on an aeroplane and everyone joins in.'

Feathering the Empty Nest

'You lose a child, you gain a sex life.'
LETTY COTTIN POGREBIN

For anyone still very much in the throes of a household dominated by its adolescent inhabitants, an empty nest may seem little more than wishful thinking. Let's face it, life with teenagers can be challenging. During the six years it takes them to get from being twelve to eighteen, you age roughly twenty. They ignore most of what you say and scoff at the rest. After all, you know nothing, you don't understand and it really isn't fair.

If it's any consolation, things have always been this way. For as long as man has been able to make written complaint, the insolence of youth has been bemoaned and bewailed by some of the greatest thinkers in history.

Here we have a couple of not just grumpy old dogs, but grumpy *ancient* dogs:

In the fifth century BC Socrates complained: 'The children love luxury. They have bad manners, contempt for authority, show disrespect for elders, and love to chatter in place of exercise.'

In the fourth century BC, Plato grumbled: 'Our youth have an insatiable desire for wealth; they have bad manners and atrocious customs regarding dressing and their hair and what garments or shoes they wear.'

And Mark Twain was man enough to admit to his own intolerable teenaged years in an article he wrote for the *Atlantic Monthly* in 1874: 'When I was a boy of fourteen, my father was so ignorant I could hardly stand to have the old man around. But when I got to be twenty-one, I was astonished at how much he had learned in seven years.'

So, take a deep breath, keep your drinks cabinet locked

and be patient: the end is nigh. And in the meantime, take some comfort from a British study that concluded that eventually we all come to appreciate everything our parents did for us. At what magic age will this happen? The standard advice used to be that you just have to keep strong until they turn twenty-two.

However, these are tough times for young people. In 2022, the average age that children in the UK moved out of their parents' home was twenty-five years old. For Londoners it's even harder, the average age there was thirty (meaning, obviously, that a huge proportion is even older than that).

So buckle up, hang in there and pray your children get well-paid jobs. In the meantime, here are a few inspirational thoughts about the beautiful relationship between children and their parents.

*'Having a child is like getting a tattoo …
on your face. You better be committed.'*

ELIZABETH GILBERT

*'Having children is like living in a frat
house: nobody sleeps, everything is broken,
and there's a lot of throwing up.'*

RAY ROMANO

'Most children threaten at times to run away from home. This is the only thing that keeps some parents going.'

PHYLLIS DILLER

'Parenthood … it's about guiding the next generation and forgiving the last.'

PETER KRAUSE

'When my kids become wild and unruly, I use a nice, safe playpen. When they're finished, I climb out.'

ERMA BOMBECK

*'You've turned into your dad the day
you put aside a thin piece of wood
specifically to stir paint with.'*

PETER KAY

*'On our 6 a.m. walk, my daughter asked where
the moon goes each morning. I let her know
it's in heaven, visiting Daddy's freedom.'*

RYAN REYNOLDS

Just the two of us

When the kids finally leave home we all react differently. Some cling to their precious offspring, sobbing wet tears onto their shoulder, wailing that life will never be the same again. Others have already picked out the new office suite and fabric swatches for their vacated room before the bags are even packed. Either way, 'empty nest syndrome' involves a major overhaul of the way of life you've settled into for the past couple of decades. More to the point, once the last of your kids leave home, there's no one to blame stuff on any more.

Letting go of the controls

Newspaper columnist Erma Bombeck's quirky take on family life kept many American parents going through the dark years of their offspring's adolescence. She had plenty to say about empty nest syndrome too, pointing out that what parents find so hard about the transition is not 'mourning the passing of all those wet towels on the floor, or the music that numbs your teeth, or even the bottle of capless shampoo dribbling down the shower drain'. The problem is something much more fundamental. 'They're upset because they've gone from supervisor of a child's life to a spectator. It's like being the vice president of the United States.'

The Advantages
of Ageing

*'What's all the fuss about being asked one's
date of birth? The answer is easy – just do as I
do and lie. As far as I know, there's no law that
says you can't pretend to be a forgetful old bag.
Live up to the expectations of John Q. Public
about elderly dottiness when it suits you.'*

MARGARET LOVE

If you find yourself looking in the mirror and realize
you've already skipped through the phase where
you look like one of your parents, and gone straight
to looking like the grandparents, you may find some
consolation in the thought that old people can basically
get away with anything. You can finally say what you
really think, insult strangers with impunity, and let it
all hang out; after all, you're a senior citizen now, so it
would be disrespectful for anyone to try to stop you.

The attendant

According to a tale related by journalist Walter Kiernan, a customer in a department store in Denmark walked into the ladies' toilets one day, only to be stared at in a very unfriendly manner by the elderly attendant when she didn't leave a tip. The woman consequently complained to the management, who decided to do a check on the toilet attendant.

It transpired that she wasn't one of the store's employees at all, but a woman who had wandered into the restroom a year previously and sat down to do a bit of knitting. Mistaking her for the attendant, customers began leaving her tips. So the woman had returned to the store every day, bringing her knitting with her.

Mistaken identity

One day, the American writer and comedian Robert Benchley was out to dinner with his son, Nathaniel.

'We went to the Trocadero,' writes Nathaniel in his memoir of his father, *Robert Benchley: A Biography*. 'When, in the course of events, we left to go home, he went to a uniformed man at the door and said, "Would you get us a taxi, please?"

'The man turned round and regarded him icily. "I'm very sorry," he said. "I happen to be a rear admiral in the United States Navy." "All right, then," said my father. "Get us a battleship."'

Don't make me wait

The actress Edith Evans was never anything if not direct. Such a quality has even greater liberty with one's increasing years. During rehearsals for what was proving to be a rather melodramatic play, Evans once said to a much younger fellow actress: 'I'm a very old lady. I may die during one of your pauses.'

'I have enjoyed greatly the second blooming ... suddenly you find – at the age of fifty, say – that a whole new life has opened before you.'

AGATHA CHRISTIE

What age do you want to be?

Bear in mind that it is perfectly OK to lie through your teeth about your real age, now that you are ancient. The art historian and novelist Anita Brookner, irritated by the constant speculation about her age which appeared in the press after she had won the Booker Prize for Fiction with *Hotel du Lac*, wrote to *The Times* to say, 'I am forty-six, and have been for some past time.' Though, as the American showman Will Rogers once said, 'Eventually you'll reach a point where you stop lying about your age and start bragging about it.' This is a good example of an old dog learning a useful new trick.

It's a hat thing

British novelist H.G. Wells is probably best remembered for such books as *The War of the Worlds* (1898) and *The History of Mr Polly* (1910), but what is perhaps less well known about him is that as he grew older, he became increasingly absent-minded ... and eccentric.

For instance, one evening, upon leaving a party he had been attending in Cambridge, he picked up someone else's hat by mistake. On discovering what he had done, however, Wells did not return the item to its rightful owner (whose name was printed inside the brim), but instead wrote him a letter.

'I stole your hat; I like your hat; I shall keep your hat. Whenever I look inside it, I shall think of you and your excellent sherry and of the town of Cambridge. I take off your hat to you.'

Oh, Carol!

According to an anecdote told by Truman Capote in *Answered Prayers*, the Hollywood actor Walter Matthau was once at a party with his wife Carol, when she overheard him talking to an elderly woman who, as Carol described her, was 'mutton dressed as lamb'.

Apparently, Walter was then overheard asking, 'How old are you?' At which point, Carol butted in and said, 'Why don't you saw off her legs and count the rings?'

Making your children feel guilty

Here's a new trick for you. One weekend, a woman decided to call her father in California because it had been quite some time since they had chatted.

The woman asked her father, 'How are you doing?'

'Not too good,' he said. 'I'm very weak.'

'Pop, why are you so weak?' the daughter asked.

'Because I haven't eaten anything in thirty-eight days,' came the reply.

The daughter then asked, 'How come you haven't eaten in thirty-eight days?'

'Because I didn't want my mouth to be filled with food when you called,' he replied.

Little accidents

When you start having little accidents of the urinary kind, it's a sure signal that the years are really creeping up on you. But this next story takes that to a whole new level. One day, the English actress Mrs Patrick Campbell, who was carrying her pet dog Moonbeam in her arms,

hailed down a London taxicab. At first, the driver didn't want to take the pair in his car, but Campbell climbed in nonetheless and ordered, 'The Empire Theatre, my man, and no nonsense!'

On the way there, however, Moonbeam disgraced himself on the floor of the cab, leading the driver to point out the large puddle now soiling his vehicle.

But Mrs Campbell wouldn't hear a word of it. 'Moonbeam didn't pee,' she said, 'I did.'

Or is it just all bad?

On his eightieth birthday, British author W. Somerset Maugham was making an after-dinner speech at a meal held in his honour at London's Garrick Club.

'There are many virtues in growing old,' he began, before stopping to gaze round the room. The pause continued with Maugham shifting restlessly from foot to foot, rearranging his notes.

Finally, he coughed and continued: 'I'm just trying to think what they are.'

Modern Life is Rubbish

*'We used to build civilizations. Now
we build shopping malls.'*

BILL BRYSON

One of the defining features of life for a long time now has been the increasingly complex efforts of the retail industry to coax us into spending more money, for smaller products of decreasing quality. If you want to see shrinkflation in action, just look at the next box of biscuits you buy. The chances are it will be the same size it used to be but the 'extra large' cookies will be much smaller than the space allotted to them, or the plastic tray that used to contain twelve cookies in a row will have been redesigned to contain a mere six, artfully arranged diagonally so as to fill the box.

We like to think we are smart enough to outwit these companies, but in the end, we are mostly just sheep-like consumers, being driven into parting with our hard-earned money, encouraged with marketing and advertising drives that act like cattle prods.

Before you know it, you are in your very own cost-of-living crisis, struggling to get your head above water, and, rather than go shopping for even more food, trying to work out how to use all the rice, lentils and spaghetti you panic-bought in the pandemic. On the bright side, all that toilet paper in the garage will last a year or two yet.

But modern shopping habits involve several new tricks that not every old dog can deal with ...

Internet shopping

We all live busy lives. Between working longer hours, hitting the gym to justify the huge annual membership fee, dropping the kids off at school and finding time to plough through thousands of hours of *Succession*, there's barely a moment to get to the shops. Especially since the pandemic, we've mostly become chemically dependent on Internet shopping. Not only is it great for essentials, it's also fabulous for buying stuff you never knew you wanted or needed. Whether you're sourcing original vinyl, baby booties from French artisans or a polystyrene coffin full of frozen steaks from an organic farm in Scotland, a world of unnecessary purchases is at your fingertips. In fact, you now spend so much of your evenings picking out reclaimed tiles on eBay that you barely have time to wonder when and where all this stuff is getting delivered.

It isn't. At least, not to your house. All you'll receive in return for your hours in front of the screen is a series of illegibly signed cards pushed through your letter box by a delivery man informing you that your hard-researched purchases are available for collection from an industrial estate five miles away.

Or worse, it was dumped on your doorstep and a passer-by has happily helped themselves to it.

'To err is human, but to really foul things up requires a computer.'

AUTHOR UNKNOWN

Loyalty cards

It's official. You have more and more loyalty cards but have no idea how many points you have accumulated or what you could do with them. This fact hasn't stopped you filling your wallet with dozens of these things and dutifully producing them every time you buy groceries, clothes, coffee or petrol. The brochure they came with seemed to indicate that using the cards was something to do with sun-drenched holidays or getting a new car but you can't be sure, as you didn't read the small print.

In fact, every penny you spend with a loyalty card equates to a large and opaque number of points – 1754.56 for example – and there are different scales for cash purchases, debit card purchases, goods on sale and so on. So if you want to know when you qualify for the new car, you will need a decent grasp of theoretical mathematics to work it out.

Like any addiction, your unflinching loyalty to your loyalty cards will eventually drive you insane as you attempt to satisfy your need for points. It will start when you are consumed with rage when you discover your partner has done a weekly shop without using the loyalty card. Then you will find yourself regularly driving around for an extra forty minutes to find the nearest supermarket rather than risk missing out on vital pointage. Finally, you will hit rock bottom and find yourself 'tilling' – the despicable practice of picking up the discarded receipts of others to add the points to your own card.

The only answer is to admit that you are hopelessly enslaved to providing marketing data to the supermarket, cut up your cards and take it one day at a time.

Cheap plastic toys

In their ongoing attempt to destabilize the West, our Chinese overlords have unleashed a torrent of plastic toys and dolls. These smiling, wall-eyed monstrosities crowd the shelves of our toy shops, supermarket checkouts and museum gift shops like a malevolent invasion force from some distant psychedelic planet.

When you were growing up you had virtually no toys. A lone Action Man, a beloved Barbie doll, maybe an Etch A Sketch or a space hopper, all made in Hong Kong and all cherished because you knew that breaking them meant no toys until your next birthday. These long-time companions have been replaced in our children's affections with a rotating gallery of faceless, bleeping bedfellows.

Your kids can barely find their pyjamas for the number of cheap plastic toys clogging up their bedrooms. You give your kids toys for being good and to stop them being bad. They used to get toys in their cereal packets, with their Happy Meals, as mementos of family trips out and to while away rainy afternoons. On birthdays and Christmas your friends join in to create a tottering mound of cheap gifts that take your children most of the day to open.

While these toys play an eminently disposable role in your kids' lives, they are absolutely indestructible in the real world. In 1992, an armada of 29,000 plastic yellow ducks, blue turtles and green frogs made in China for the US firm The First Years Inc, were washed overboard in the eastern Pacific. Since then they have travelled many thousands of miles, some landing in Hawaii and others spending several years frozen in the Arctic ice. They have floated over the site where the *Titanic* sank and even outlasted the ship which was originally carrying them.

With this in mind, every parent can look forward to finding disembodied Marvel figures and random Funko Pop! toys in suit pockets and handbags for many years to come.

Coffee shops

Coffee shops are everywhere these days. You can't turn a corner without seeing a Starbucks, a Coffee Republic, a Costa or a Caffé Nero, often right next to one another and all staffed by cheery students with baseball caps, nose rings and burns all over their forearms. In addition, we now have an escalating level of hipster pop-up shops and shacks, all selling a bewildering range of drinks, including monstrosities like almond frappés and bubble tea.

Such is the ubiquity of coffee shops that the companies have been forced to seek new real estate, erecting them in hospitals, petrol stations, even a job centre. In fact, it's only a matter of time before they start building them on the only free ground remaining – inside each other.

Remember, coffee is no longer simply coffee. It's a statement, a fashion accessory; it is, in fact, part of a

'look'. US comedian Maria Bamford sees it as a sign of a generation with way too many civil liberties. She says it's often the moment you witness someone making an outrageously extravagant coffee order that you find yourself asking, 'Hey, maybe we have too much freedom in the United States?'

You can remember a time when coffee came in one size and was either black or white. Now you have to decide if you fancy an espresso, a mocha or latte and whether it's tall (big), grande (huge) or venti (vast). You will also need to decide whether you want a defibrillator-like extra shot or heart-stopping whipped cream. Also on offer are marshmallows and a dash from a selection of tempting bottles stacked behind the counter that look like booze but taste like cough syrup. And is there anyone in the world who truly knows the difference between a flat white and an Americano with hot milk?

Are coffee choices a new trick we don't need to learn?

Organic food

What's going on with childhood today? All you can remember when you were a child is bland food, uninspiring toys, early bedtimes and an all-pervasive fear of adults. Your kids treat the world with the unchecked self-regard and wilful abuse of their fellow man more commonly found in the palaces of dictators. Desperate for an explanation, you convince yourself that the borderline psychotic behaviour manifested by your offspring must be caused by something in their turkey twizzlers. So you decide to go organic.

For food to be certified organic, it must be produced without the use of synthetic pesticides, fertilizers, antibiotics or food additives – and as you'd prefer these chemicals were used to clean your kitchen rather than to line the inside of your stomach, this sounds good. The organic movement claims food grown as nature intended has benefits both for the environment and personal health, and even that it has higher levels of minerals than its non-organic counterparts. Again – it sounds great. Finally, organic food is not irradiated. In practical terms this means fresh food will probably go off before you get a chance to cook it. In short, you'll be spending a lot of time in your local organic superstore.

The organic superstore looks pretty much like a normal supermarket if you tripled the prices and didn't bother to paint the fittings.

But what really grates is that every single product on the shelves has a story printed on the back. Usually this is about how old-timers Mom & Pop Organic decide to knit a range of toilet paper on their smallholding or, more accurately, how Old Jed Wholeearth's pasta sauce tasted so good that he demolished his bankrupt farm and built a factory on the site to produce it in industrial quantities using tomatoes imported from China.

And is any child ever truly grateful when you offer them the healthiest, safest, grittiest, greenest meal they have ever seen? Or do they just take one of those frozen lasagnes out of the freezer and put it in the microwave?

On a side note, the saddest group of children I've ever seen were the little band of friends being led down the high street by a cheery ecomother thanking them for coming on their little 'vegan adventure' that afternoon. It was truly tragic, as they craned their necks to stare wistfully at the cupcakes in the nearest non-organic, non-vegan shop window display.

Supermarkets

Are you one of the few hold-outs resisting giving in to the convenience of online shopping? If so, good for you, at least if you are supporting the local high street in the process. But you are only kidding yourself if you are going to the supermarket instead.

When you were growing up there was only one supermarket – now called a superstore. It was in the centre of town and everybody went to it for their weekly shop. Then the big grocery chains, spurred on by hundreds of thousands of pounds of market research and a desire for unchecked expansion, started messing with the size of their stores, leaving you feeling more like Alice in Wonderland than a hungry punter. There's probably method in this madness but what do you know? You're just a customer who's trying to buy a loaf of bread.

The superstore sells things that you never previously associated with the supermarket like TVs, kitchen utensils and sports equipment. Arriving at the supermarket you become lost in the aisles as you search for your seeded batch. Overwhelmed by the sheer volume of stuff on sale, you panic-buy enough canned goods to keep you going for a year. At least you'll be in good stead when the next pandemic strikes.

'Anyone who believes the competitive spirit in America is dead has never been in a supermarket when the cashier opens another checkout line.'

ANN LANDERS

Unexpected item in the bagging area

In theory, a machine should be more efficient at serving us in a shop than a human being, especially when that human being is a heavily pierced teenager in an ill-fitting nylon uniform with a cider hangover. In practice, this is not the case because the person operating that machine is you.

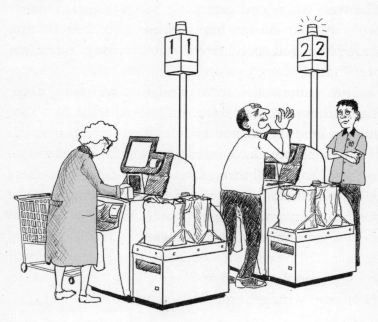

The fact that you are the weakest link in this chain is the last thing on your mind as you jump the long supermarket queue and confidently bowl up to the automated checkout. All you will be doing is taking neatly packaged items from your basket of groceries, passing them in front of a laser scanner then placing them in a plastic bag. It's something you've watched the human cashiers do a million times with the kind of 'please kill me' look in their eyes that can only mean the task is far from challenging.

The da Vinci barcode

However, when you get going, it's a different story. None of your chosen items have the barcode in the same place. You spend five minutes turning each item over to find where to scan. When you finally locate the barcode, some will scan easily with a satisfying beep, while others require careful smoothing of the wrapper or being held at the correct angle. Then you pick a bunch of bananas. These have no barcode at all and need to be weighed. You scroll through an endless series of menus more reminiscent of finding a document on the office intranet than a visit to the shops.

You give up and look plaintively around the shop for help. The heavily pierced teen – who has now served the four people who were originally in front of you in the queue – trudges around the counter and assists you by nonchalantly using one hand to key a secret code at incredible speed.

Things look like they are on the up until a foolish attempt to get another bag from the stand results in the computer announcing there is an unexpected item in the bagging area. To the designers of these machines this phrase may mean something, but to you – who doesn't know what the item is or where officially constitutes the bagging area – it is one of the most oblique string of words in the language.

Waiting for the man

What is clear is that you can't scan any more items until it's sorted, which means waiting for the return of the teen who has managed to serve another three customers in the interim. Before you can splutter a series of excuses, the teen has swiftly and efficiently reset the machine and – without making eye contact – run through the rest of your groceries at the same time.

Red-faced and flustered, you hustle out of the shop and resolve to order your groceries online in future.

Yep, you can't teach an old dog new tricks.

*'A bargain is something you can't use
at a price you can't resist.'*

FRANKLIN P. JONES

Contactless shopping

Happily, the retail industry is here to help. You can now shop in a store where you log in with your membership card, pick up a basket, wander round choosing your items, and then simply walk out. Meanwhile, the software has been tracking your movements, itemizing your purchases and registering the prices. Then, once it has added them all up, it can take whatever it fancies directly from your bank account behind your back. Brilliant.

Cold hard cash

Most of us are increasingly used to tapping our cards when we check out of a store. However, using debit cards the old-fashioned way can be useful when shopping. Putting aside the nerve-racking few minutes you have to endure as you keep entering your date of birth rather than your PIN number, it does force you to actually look at the payment device in order to enter it, which means you do at least know how much you spent, even if keeping track of how much you spend in the entire day would require more mental arithmetic and willpower than you are capable of.

Then having triumphantly succeeded in using your debit card, the teenager behind you in the queue merely waves their phone at the scanner and wanders off without their receipt.

No wonder young people can't save up for houses, you think, before remembering that the real reason is that property is now so eye-wateringly expensive that your children will still be living with you at the age of fifty-two. And not only that, you've turned into the kind of grumpy old dog who blames them for it.

Parking meters

There is also the question of how you get to the high street in the first place. Cars are great for getting from place to place but they are useless if you can't stop at your destination and get out. Unfortunately, armed with the triple excuse of health, safety and increased traffic flow, your council is hell-bent on making this a reality. If you are forced to pull over because your back seat is on fire, you will be spotted on camera and fined remotely.

And if you are considering pulling into a parking bay, think again. As part of a plan to make all convenient services less convenient in the name of convenience, parking bays became an active hazard as soon as their meters stopped taking real money.

That's right: you now need a mobile phone, an app and an online account with a sinister automated payment bot to park your car. So rather than dropping a few coins in the meter and popping into the shops, you discover that you have to spend ten minutes walking up and down the road trying to find the bay reference number, then another ten minutes trying to remember your car's registration number, before working out that it is written on the number plate.

All this nets the council a tidy sum. But if you were planning on giving up, parking the car in your back garden and taking the bus, you can think again. They don't take cash any more either.

'A real patriot is the fellow who gets a parking ticket and rejoices that the system is working.'

BILL VAUGHAN

Charity muggers

Another peril of the high street these days is charity muggers or 'chuggers'. But let's face it, they can get you anywhere. Every time you open your email you are confronted by an announcement that yet another of your paunchy, middle-aged friends is attempting a breathtaking feat of stupidity using the notional excuse of raising money for charity. While it might be their

choice to freeze to death on the side of Kilimanjaro or suffer a heart attack on the nineteenth mile of the Copenhagen Marathon, the bottom line is that you are going to have to fund their mid-life crisis. While you can just about bring yourself to pledge money to enable this madness, what really gets your blood up is that your money will be going to yet another charity which you have never heard of and have no interest in.

Stand and deliver

With the charities putting so much time and effort into finding new and innovative ways to siphon off your money, it would come as no surprise if they decided that it would be quicker and easier to stop you in the street and demand that you turn out the contents of your pockets ... which of course they already do. You can barely walk across a railway platform, through a subway or across a shopping centre without being leapt upon by a pensioner in a sash shaking a plastic goblet or a cheery student with a clipboard and sheaf of direct debit forms.

Really it's all a matter of balance. And the balance is so much in favour of the charities that you have come to the conclusion that it might be easier to sign over your entire pay cheque to them in the first place, leaving you free to conduct a series of sponsored moonwalks and skydives to raise the necessary funds to buy food and groceries. It would certainly be more fun, but, as an old dog, do you really want to have to learn such new tricks?

Victims of Modernity

'The correct assumption is that what individuals have learned by age twenty-one will begin to become obsolete five to ten years later and will have to be replaced – or at least refurbished – by new learning, new skills, new knowledge.'

PETER DRUCKER

We always knew the world we lived in would change as we grew older; we had science fiction and *Tomorrow's World* to teach us that. However, does it have to keep changing so damned fast? By the time we have got used to something new, it has changed, been cancelled or demolished. Remember when Windows 3.0 was the future? Remember when there were rural bus services? Remember when employees had rights? Remember when there were only three (or maybe four) TV channels?

There is so much new stuff, we are chasing our tails trying to keep up. And in the meantime, there have been some sad losses, which, as old dogs, we can only mourn.

Useful shops on the high street

A couple of decades ago you could still get pretty much anything you wanted on the high street, or even in a single branch of Woolworths. Which is, of course, now extinct. These days it is all nail bars, hairdressers, the dreaded coffee shops and the kind of pound shops whose supplies seem to have come out of a skip.

The haberdashers? Driven out of business by competition from the Internet. The DIY store? Driven out of business by the DIY superstore on the industrial estate, where you can be served the wrong item by gormless teenagers rather than asking the sensible bloke behind the counter what you actually need if you are going to try to put a shelf up.

The family restaurant that served old-school lunches and Black Forest gateau? Replaced by a chicken shop, which is frequented by already overweight youths. The independent café? Driven out of business by a combination of coffee chains and the kinds of independent hipster pop-up stores that sell trendy Vietnamese street food at boutique prices that would once have bought you a three-course meal.

No wonder high streets are in decline; there may come a time when they are also on the list of 'Things you remember existing when you were younger'.

Newspapers

For the past decade or more, we have listened to doom-and-gloom stories about how mainstream media is failing and that soon newspapers will be a thing of the past. You don't really read the newspaper any more. They are full of stories about children being eaten by Rottweilers, celebrity marriages and endless stories about the decline in newspaper ad revenue. They are simply too depressing to bother with.

Arguably, the real reason why newspapers are in trouble is that some bright spark thought it would be a good idea to give them away. While you don't claim to be the world's greatest economist, even you can see that employing people to write a newspaper, printing the copies and delivering them all over the country must incur considerable costs, so that handing them out like curry-house flyers is daft.

Meanwhile, the so-called highbrow newspapers are in deep trouble; the Sunday edition which used to be a bundle of highly designed supplements and specials has now been reduced to a smaller size, with only two or three flimsy extras, and covers clearly designed by either an intern or an AI.

The park café

When you were a child, the café in the park was up there with hospital bins and open sewage overflows as one of the premier urban biohazards. A failing greasy spoon that was part urinal and part unsanctioned needle exchange, even parents as disinterested and incompetent as yours knew not to take their kids there. But the café in the park has undergone something of a renaissance. Nowadays it's a deli with a grassed play area, nice wooden tables and a queue of sleep-deprived yummy mummies in outsized designer shades snaking out the door. It's all because some bright spark realized that the trick to drawing in the middle-class punters was not cheap and cheerful fare with free corkage on super-strength lagers, but launching a wilfully expensive eatery that would make the prices in a Michelin-starred restaurant seem reasonable.

With such a captive audience, it is surprising no one worked this out sooner. If you're a parent with young kids, you will spend up to 50 per cent of your life in

the park. The prospect of spending four hours pushing swings and feigning interest in rabid-looking squirrels fills you with such horror that the ten minutes reprieve offered by spending fifteen pounds on a coffee and two pastries for the kids seems like a bargain.

This being the case, why do the shark-eyed restaurateurs even bother with nice food? Come rain or shine, you will be in the park, traipsing around after your pretentiously named offspring who behave like a bunch of mental patients after a smash-and-grab raid on a scooter shop.

You could argue that middle-class parents demand a higher quality of al fresco fare, but the real reason for the growth of this culinary highway robbery is much simpler – the promise of health. If you want to keep your spouse off your back, you can't take the kids to McDonald's. Besides, what's the point of the café owners installing an expensive deep fat fryer when they can charge you five pounds for an organic cheese sandwich with no butter?

The local pub

Have you tried going to your local pub lately? Maybe you stopped going when they banned smoking, and you realized that the smoke had been covering up the smell of stale beer and urine, or maybe your life has been revolving around dinner parties for a while.

In the unlikely event it hasn't been converted into a mega coffee shop, or block of flats, you'll find your local pub has been refurbished, no longer takes cash, has a blisteringly expensive gastro menu, and, rather than the old blokes you used to say hello to in the corner, the customers are all unfriendly middle-class groups sipping spritzers while wasting £100 on some vegan steak and quinoa or mushroom fandango.

There are no young people as none of them drink any more. There isn't even a fruit machine or dartboard. Somehow, when you weren't looking, the world you once knew has been swept away, and it's never coming back.

Welcome to the brave new world.

The sandwich shop

Possibly the lowest circle of hell is reserved for the founders of franchises that specialize in sandwiches. Once upon a time there were the kinds of sandwich shops, mostly run by Italians, where the fillings were all on display and the owner would make a sandwich up for you to order. The coffee was decent, from an old-school espresso machine, and the cakes were personally baked by the owner's family.

Have you tried to find one lately? The reason they disappeared is those repulsive sandwich chains, where the sandwiches are mass-produced by zero-hours workers in a factory miles away, and the coffee is insipid bilge.

If you want to do one thing to save the planet, I suggest boycotting every single chain of restaurants, cafés and bars, and only patronizing whichever independent alternatives you have left in your area. Otherwise we face a bleak future of corporate, bland, cynical food and drink, in which you'll be lucky ever to find a Scotch egg again.

Final Destination

*'You can spend your whole life trying
to be popular, but at the end of the day,
the size of the crowd at your funeral will
be largely dictated by the weather.'*

FRANK SKINNER

Middle age is the time when you first face the fact that you are mortal after all. Coming to terms with this can send many of us reeling for a while, turning once more to the trappings of our former days, clutching at the illusion of eternal youth for a little while longer. But no amount of fast cars, younger partners or macrobiotic diets is going to alter the fact that in the end, we're all leaving through the same door.

There aren't many new tricks to be learned about our final destination, but as old dogs we can maybe learn to laugh about it.

You can't take it with you

Maybe it's time to start to think about how you want to be remembered. It's a good thing to be proud of your work. A dying trait, some might argue. But thinking up bizarre ways to take your work with you to the grave is perhaps a sign that your work-home balance needs a little readjustment.

In 1970 an organic chemist and food storage technician from Cincinnati named Frederic Bauer designed and patented the iconic Pringles tube container. When he died at the age of eighty-four, his family honoured his last wish: they buried his ashes in a Pringles can.

Meanwhile, comic book writer, editor and genius Mark Gruenwald, of Marvel Comics, died suddenly of a heart attack in 1996, at the age of just forty-two. Known in life as a practical joker, his final request involved family and colleagues in a uniquely bizarre act. Gruenwald's wish was granted: his cremated remains were mixed in with the ink for a print run of the trade collection of Mark's finest work, *Squadron Supreme*.

Finally, Gene Roddenberry, the creator of the *Star Trek* TV series, wanted nothing more than for his ashes to be sent into space. When he died, his remains were taken up by a Spanish satellite and shot into the atmosphere to orbit the planet for eternity.

Mortality

Damon Wayans Sr is a highly successful writer and *New York Times* best-selling novelist with no apparent cause for feeling the age-related blues. However, as he explained, mid-life crises can have very little to do with where you're at with your career and a whole lot to do with realizing you have very little time left to worry about getting old.

'A mid-life crisis is the day that a man looks in the mirror and realizes he's no longer invincible. You see death in the reflection. That Grim Reaper looking at you going, "I got you in twenty years." And you try to fight it. You try to work out, but you start seeing that your chest turns into breasts.'

Having the last laugh

Writing your last will and testament is a sombre process. But many look upon it as an opportunity to make their lasting impression on the world. Take Iowa attorney T.M. Zink, for instance, who died in 1930. In life, he was incensed that women could pursue an education beyond high school. He decided to leave a legacy that would be his parting gift to the misogynist cause. He placed $35,000 into trust for seventy-five years, long enough, he estimated, for it to have accumulated enough interest to build a substantial men-only library, a womanless learning zone which he stipulated should carry a warning over every entrance: 'No Women Allowed'.

Thankfully Zink's daughter, Margaret Becker, to whom he had bequeathed just $5, successfully contested the will on the grounds that it constituted 'an insult to the womanhood of America, a libel and a slander against public morals'.

> *'I thought about killing myself. But I went on holiday to Belgium instead.'*
>
> **STEPHEN FRY**

No laughing matter

Of course, mourning rituals are deeply ingrained in specific cultures. One bizarre advert for a European life insurance policy that went viral online showed a group of grinning adults, all smartly dressed in suits and ties, throwing a man in the air repeatedly as they merrily sang, 'For He's a Jolly Good Fellow'. As the camera panned back, we saw a white-satin lined coffin surrounded by lilies and realized that the fellow in question was a stiff. The voice-over urged us all to take out this particular policy on the basis that 'your family will love you for it'. The original ad had apparently been banned – hardly surprising, given the flippant way it dealt with death and bereavement.

But it's certainly true that in the West we are often guilty of a somewhat restrained grieving process. Actress and comedian Victoria Wood summed it up succinctly, pointing out that in India, when a man dies, his widow throws herself on the funeral pyre. Over here, said Wood, it's more like: 'Fifty ham baps, Beryl – you slice, I'll butter.'

It's good to have a plan

Scottish people are known for their straight-talking attitude to life and death. The nation that advises you to live life to the full on the basis that you're dead a long time, is perhaps most famously embodied in the person of much-loved comedian Billy Connolly. And this philosophy is right there in Connolly's joke: 'Two guys are talking and one says to the other, "What would you do if the end of the world was in three minutes' time?" The other one says, "I'd shag everything that moved ... What would you do?" And he says, "I'd stand perfectly still."'

A final act of defiance

For anyone who finds fulfilment in adhering to the fine print in life, planning your death can be a golden opportunity. We all know the type: the guy who stores his socks balled up in neat pairs, meticulously sorts his recycling and files his tax returns a week early. Rob Brydon, the Welsh actor and comedian who excels at playing exactly this type, sums it up. 'I plan to put my ashes, while still hot, into one of those green wheelie bins. That'll show 'em.'

Honouring the dead

There are as many ways to honour your loved ones as there are families. A well-thought-out eulogy, a beautiful headstone, or ashes scattered under a favourite rose bush; the list is endless and highly personal. But Rolling Stone Keith Richards admitted to his very own brand of memorial for his late father. 'He was cremated and I couldn't resist grinding him up with a bit of blow,' he said. 'My dad wouldn't have cared … it went down pretty well, and I'm still alive.'

'When I die, I want it to be on my hundredth birthday, in my beach house on Maui, and I want my husband to be so upset he has to drop out of college.'

PERI GILPIN (ROZ), IN *FRASIER*

Don't fear the reaper

Death's a drag, isn't it? As if it weren't already miserable enough, the heavy mahogany of the traditional coffin, draped in lilies and lined with satin, is enough to put even the most incurable optimist on a proper downer. So why not decide now to tackle that last taboo head-on? A palliative care foundation based in Singapore staged a competition in 2010 for designers to come up with 'happy coffins'.

YOU CAN'T TEACH AN OLD DOG NEW TRICKS

There were more than seven hundred whimsical entries from all over the world, most of which threw a finger to traditions of sombre mourning. One entry, a French-designed coffin, resembled a crate of wine complete with a single bottle nestling in among the packing straw. A label dangling from the neck of the bottle read, 'Special Vintage'. Perfect for anyone who thinks they're premier cru.

'The trouble with quotes about death is that 99.9% of them are made by people who are still alive.'

JOSHUA BURNS